DOMIN

✺ DOMINIC ✺

edited and introduced
by

Vladimir J. Koudelka OP

English version
by

Consuelo Fissler OP and **Simon Tugwell** OP

with illustrations by
Juliet Pannett MBE

edited by

Simon Tugwell OP

DARTON · LONGMAN + TODD

First published in Great Britain in 1997 by
Darton, Longman and Todd Ltd
1 Spencer Court
140–142 Wandsworth High Street
London SW18 4JJ

First published as *Dominikus* by Walter-Verlag AG, Olten

Nihil obstat: Basil Cole OP and Alfred Wilder OP
Imprimi potest: Timothy Radcliffe OP
Magister Ordinis Fratrum Praedicatorum
8 February 1994

ISBN 0–232–52068–2

A catalogue record for this book is available
from the British Library

Phototypeset in 10½/13½pt Times by Intype London Ltd
Printed and bound in Great Britain by
Redwood Books, Trowbridge, Wiltshire

CONTENTS

Part One: INTRODUCTION

Part Two: TEXTS

PREFACE
TO THE GERMAN EDITION

Almost everyone today has some picture of Francis of Assisi. By comparison his contemporary, Dominic, is almost unknown or else he is 'known' wrongly. The high evangelical ideal of Francis and the romantic aspects of his personality appeal to poets and artists and idealists, though at the same time they leave him vulnerable to misrepresentation and misunderstanding. He has often been appropriated or misappropriated by short-lived movements and ideologies, with scant regard for his real concerns. The life and work of Dominic are much less likely to stir people's emotions – they seem too prosaic for that. To get to know him properly requires a fundamental study of the sources and of the religious, political and economic situation of the end of the twelfth century and the beginning of the thirteenth. This is all the more necessary because he has left us no writings to provide a basis for the construction of a systematic doctrine or to furnish precise instructions for our own religious life or perhaps rouse our own religious sensibilities. He was a man of great spiritual experience, and he had a profound effect on people, which enabled him to be of service to the faith, the church and the world of his time. His teaching was embodied in his compelling personality and his example, which remained stamped on his followers, who developed his 'teaching' and his thinking and his programme, in the process releasing new forces, which are still operative today. Dominic had the grace of the spoken, not the written word, but his word was backed by the harmonious richness of his personality, by his experience of God and by his practical wisdom. All these elements can be seen clearly in the sources. In this book, for the first time, the various primary sources for his life are arranged thematically so as to bring out for the reader this harmony between Dominic's personality and his work. It was his achievement to take up the elements of the contemporary 'Apostolic Life' movements and work them into a concrete synthesis, which resulted in the creation of new structures for the religious life and for the apostolic life, which could then reveal its true fruitfulness. The introductions are intended to help the reader to understand the complex situation of Dominic's time and to judge for himself or herself what service Dominic rendered to the church of his age, and indeed to the universal church and to human culture.

Vladimir J. Koudelka OP

PREFACE
TO THE ENGLISH EDITION

All historians who are concerned with St Dominic or with his period are indebted to Father Koudelka for a series of fascinating and important articles which he wrote during his years in the Dominican Historical Institute in Rome and for an excellent edition of the pertinent letters and official documents from the lifetime of St Dominic. It is now many years since Father Koudelka retired from the Historical Institute to devote himself to other work, but in this present book he has given us a distillation of the historical figure of Dominic which his own detailed research did so much to enliven and fill out. It is a valuable, if sometimes controversial, contribution to the efforts of scholars to understand the personality of Dominic and the circumstances in which the Dominican Order took shape, circumstances which mark the whole of its subsequent history.

On a few points of detail Father Koudelka has kindly authorised me to make some small changes and occasional editorial comments, in the light of more recent historical and textual studies, but the English version of this book is, in all essentials, a reproduction in English of his original German text. I have tried to avoid doing anything which would change *his* vision, *his* interpretation of the story. Although on some questions my own research has led me to different, sometimes significantly different, conclusions about what happened, Father Koudelka's work has long been a particular inspiration to me and it is a real pleasure to me to present *his* Dominic to a wider readership.

The English version of the general Introduction and of the

comments on particular sections of the book was produced by Sr Consuelo Fissler and myself in collaboration. The selection of texts from the thirteenth-century sources was translated by me from the original Latin, in many cases on the basis of new editions which have been published since Father Koudelka finished working on the book or which are still in process of being completed. One of the more daunting tasks which Father Koudelka undertook in the Historical Institute was that of producing a scholarly edition of the last major thirteenth-century biography of Dominic, by Dietrich of Apolda; he was unable to do more than make a beginning and the project eventually found its way on to my shoulders, and it subsequently expanded to become a plan to prepare critical editions of all the main medieval writings on St Dominic. It is in the light of the work in progress towards the realisation of this somewhat ambitious scheme that I have translated the texts selected by Father Koudelka.

The translations in the original German edition of this book were not made by Father Koudelka himself, and in some cases an accidental confusion resulted in citations from more than one author getting scrambled up together. I have unscrambled them again. This has necessitated a slight rearrangment of some of the material. Thus in the text which is number 110 in the German I have eliminated a passage from Guillaume de Puylaurens which had got mixed up with a far more important text from Pierre des Vaux-de-Cernai, and number 115 I have split into two, to separate Puylaurens from Cernai. In numbers 172–173 I have cut out some of the unnecessary verbiage in which Constantine of Orvieto delighted; in so doing, I have followed the example of that much more sober writer, Humbert of Romans. On, I think, two occasions I have included a few extra sentences from the original source, where it seemed to me to be useful. Occasionally a few words have been added to the translation, in square brackets, to make the sense clearer. In the case of the *Nine Ways of Prayer of St Dominic* I have followed Father Koudelka in keeping the whole text, even though that now turns out to contain two anecdotes which were not included in the edition used by Father Koudelka. I have also added three new texts (nos. 14, 95 and 115). On the other hand, I have suppressed most of 124, since the same passage was quoted in full in 53. Otherwise the texts given here are the same as those found in the German. For convenience of reference, the numbers in the English version correspond as follows to those in the German:

German	English
1–13	1–13
–	14
14–93	15–94
–	95
94–112	96–114
–	115
113–114	116–117
115	118–119
116–180	120–184

Biblical references are generally identified in the text, following the practice of Father Koudelka, even though these are usually not specified in the original Latin. The numbering of the Psalms follows that of the Latin Vulgate.

The main innovation in the English version of the book is a new Introduction to the Sources which I have written, at the request of the publishers, to replace most of the first section of the original German Introduction, and an annotated Index of Sources. I have also revised and adapted the Bibliography.

It remains to express my gratitude to the Paulist Press, which has kindly allowed me to re-use some translations which were published in my volume, *Early Dominicans*, which appeared in 1982 in their series, Classics of Western Spirituality, and to Dominican Sources for permission to adapt some passages from my translation of Jordan of Saxony which appeared in that collection, also in 1982. I am, of course, profoundly grateful to Father Koudelka himself for the support he has given to this

English version of his work. A special word of thanks must go to my old friend, Juliet Pannett, who most generously undertook to provide new illustrations for the *Nine Ways of Prayer of St Dominic*. I must also declare my appreciation of the encouragement given me by several people to whom I showed the translation when it was first made, and of the perseverance with which Darton, Longman and Todd have overcome the curious obstacles which for so long delayed the publication of this book.

Simon Tugwell OP
Dominican Historical Institute, Rome

TABLE OF DATES

1216 (16 July)	Innocent III dies in Perugia and on 18 July Cencio Savelli becomes pope as Honorius III.
1216 (autumn)	Dominic goes to Rome from Toulouse and asks Honorius III to confirm his Order of Preachers.
1216 (22 Dec.)	Honorius III takes Dominic's diocesan Order of Preachers under his protection and confirms Dominic and his brethren as religious living under the Rule of St Augustine.
1217 (21 Jan.)	Honorius III confirms preaching as the goal of Dominic's order and gives the name 'preachers' to him and his brethren in Toulouse.
1217 (Aug. 15)	Dominic sends most of his friars away to Paris or to Spain.
1218 (early)	Dominic is in Rome, from where he sends some of his friars to Bologna.
1218 (summer)	Dominic goes from Rome to Spain.
1219	Dominic goes from Spain to Paris via Toulouse, and then to Bologna.
1219 (Nov.)	Dominic is at the papal court in Viterbo and receives the official commission to reform the Roman nuns and unite them in the newly built monastery at San Sisto.
1220 (May)	The first general chapter of the order in Bologna gives the order new constitutions.
1220	During the rest of the summer Dominic pays two visits to Milan and, in connection with the second of them, makes a tour of Lombardy with some of his friars.
1221 (Jan.)	Dominic is in Rome.
1221 (28 Feb.)	Dominic establishes the reformed monastery for nuns at the basilica of San Sisto in Rome.
1221 (end of May)	Second general chapter in Bologna.
1221	After the general chapter Dominic goes to Venice, making a preaching tour on his way.
1221 (6 Aug.)	Dominic dies in Bologna.
1234 (3 July)	Dominic is canonised by Gregory IX.

INTRODUCTION TO THE SOURCES

Simon Tugwell OP

As Father Koudelka remarks, in many ways we are particularly well informed about St Dominic. But the story has to be pieced together from a wide range of disparate sources. Many of the essential facts are known to us from official documents and more or less contemporary chronicles, such as Pierre des Vaux-de-Cernai's history of the Albigensian campaign, in which the author himself had taken part, or from later, local chronicles, such as that of Guillaume de Puylaurens for the south of France and, in Bologna, the chronicle of the monastery of St Agnes. After all, for most of his adult life Dominic was a public figure, involved in public affairs. But we do not have the kind of sources which would give us a coherent and more intimate picture of the man himself. In particular, none of the letters we know he used to write to his brethren survive; the only writings we possess from him are two purely formal letters, and a letter of exhortation to the Dominican nuns in Madrid. If we would become acquainted with his personality, we must learn to recognise him in different kinds of material supplied by writings of many sorts, which were not primarily intended to serve this particular purpose.

It may seem strange, but it is the case that the early Dominicans made no systematic effort to compile anything like a proper biography of their founder. They were surely not inappreciative of him, but, for whatever reason, they did not at first feel compelled to do for Dominic what the early Franciscans did for Francis. And this has a great deal to do with the very special role of Dominic in the development of his order.

Without Dominic, the Order of Preachers as we know it would certainly not have come into existence. But the order was not simply his personal brainchild and he was not, and never claimed to be, its sole inspiration or even the primary embodiment of its nature and ideals. Francis, even when he tried to avoid it, was always at the centre of the stage; to a considerable extent he had to be seen as standing over against his followers, as their model and judge. It is quite natural that after his death people started writing about him with a sharp focus on his own individual exploits and character. But Dominic was never alone on the stage, nor did he normally choose to be at the centre of the stage. Throughout most of his life he was involved in other people's schemes and activities, and it was always with his brethren and with the authorities of the church that he shaped the nascent Order of Preachers. To focus too sharply on him as an individual is in fact to distort the focus. The true story of Dominic is a story of his engagement in and interaction with events in which the presence and contribution of many other people is essential.

A prominent place in almost all the thirteenth-century writings about Dominic is accorded to Bl. Reginald of Orleans, and he illustrates well the reason why the order's historiography seems at first sight so reluctant to give pride of place to Dominic. Before he had ever heard of Dominic, Reginald had already conceived the idea of renouncing everything to become a preacher. What Dominic did was to attract him to seek the fulfilment of this dream in the Dominican Order. As soon as Reginald was free to join the order, Dominic put him in charge of his as yet not very successful foundation in Bologna. That is to say, Reginald received no 'Dominican formation'. Dominic accepted him as a ready-made Dominican. And it was Reginald more than anyone else who built up and formed the community in Bologna, which soon became one of the two major centres of the order.

Dominic then sent Reginald to Paris where, in the short time before he died, he received into the order the man destined to succeed Dominic as Master of the Order, Bl. Jordan of Saxony. Jordan too must have been seen as another ready-made Dominican. Less than two months after he joined the order he was chosen to be one of the four representatives of Paris at the general chapter of 1220. A year later he was nominated provincial of Lombardy, and in 1222 he became Master of the Order.

If it is obviously correct, in one sense, to call Dominic the founder of the Order of Preachers, we must nevertheless recognise that people like Reginald and, later, Jordan made their own distinctive contributions to the shaping of that order and that Dominic himself wished this to be so. In the birth of the order, we may say, Dominic was the midwife rather than the progenitor. There was something waiting to come to birth in the church as a whole, and Dominic was the providential agent who so splendidly and so tactfully presided over its emergence into the world and its initial formation. If the order is indelibly stamped with the imprint of Dominic's personality, this is not because he imposed or sought to impose his own ideas and temperament on it, but because he imparted to it his own sense of the dynamism of God's providence and his immense confidence in God and in the helpers and companions God gave him.

In the all-important years between the first institutionalisation of the preaching of Dominic and his associates in 1215 and Dominic's death in 1221 we get only occasional glimpses of Dominic's own thoughts. What we have instead, however, is an extraordinary succession of papal bulls, whose significance was impressively brought out by Father Koudelka. The voice that emerges with more and more clarity in these bulls is simultaneously that of Pope Honorius III and that of Dominic. It is not that Dominic was hiding behind the authority of the pope, or that the pope had become a pawn in Dominic's hands; the two men were quite sincerely working together to create something in the church.

Similarly, as the time approached for the first general chapter, in 1220, at which the new order was to create a constitutional framework suitable to its own distinctive nature and purpose, we know that Dominic talked about his own ideas and mentioned things that he wanted to be included in the Constitutions. Some of his ideas were accepted, others were not. But once the actual chapter began, we are left in the dark as to his personal role in its legislative work. It was not he who wrote the Constitutions, it was the chapter. The brethren and he together constituted a new voice; and that was what he desired. Thus the early Constitutions of the order are an important clue to the sort of man we are dealing with precisely because they do not unambiguously reflect his own thoughts and ideas.

Jordan had met Dominic before and he was one of the people who worked with him at the general chapter of 1220, but he cannot have known him all that well. Nevertheless he understood very clearly how the story of Dominic must be told. As Master of the Order, he presented his own picture of the beginnings of the order in his *Libellus*, the first work of Dominican historiography, probably issued, in considerable haste, in the early months of 1233, against the background of the new popular interest in Dominic generated by the flamboyant, thaumaturgical preaching of John of Vicenza, who was popularising the idea of the sanctity and miracle-working powers of Dominic on the basis of a vision he claimed to have had. Many of the brethren, including Jordan himself, evidently had mixed feelings about John. He was undoubtedly doing great work, but his highly individualistic and charismatic way of operating won him, for a time, such power that he was in effect answerable to no one and exempt from the control of pope and general chapter alike. A Dominic canonised against this background could turn out to be rather compromised. Not least, he would be a typical local wonder-working relic, rather than the father of a worldwide Order of Preachers. It is surely to redress the picture that Jordan published his *Libellus*, which is an extraordinary work, fitting into no proper literary category. It has some elements in common with a life of a saint and other elements in common with a religious chronicle; yet it is neither hagiography nor chronicle. But one thing does emerge very clearly, and that is the author's concern to present Dominic as a *member* of his order, as well as its father and first Master, and as a man whose story can only be told in conjunction with that of many other people, not least that of the man who was his bishop, when he was a canon of Osma, Diego of Azebes, who is presented by Jordan as taking the initiative in most of the events which led to the founding of the Order of Preachers. Jordan certainly did not want to minimise the significance of Dominic. The long and beautiful prayer he composed to the saint after his canonisation shows his own deep personal devotion to him. But he did not want 'Saint Dominic' to be a distortion of the historical and providential reality of the man Dominic and his genuine role. This explains the disconcertingly casual way in which he alludes to Dominic in the encyclical he wrote shortly after the dramatic events of the translation of Dominic's body at the general chapter of 1233, in which he exhorts the brethren to be faithful to the 'ancient paths by which our predecessors hastened to their rest', and then declares that 'our father Dominic was surely one of these'. At all costs, Dominic must not be isolated on a pedestal apart from his order. Even if he was now no longer buried under the feet of his brethren, as he had himself wanted to be, his supreme genius to be *part* of something must not be obscured.

Although the *Libellus*, as it stands, cannot have been compiled before 1232–1233, it is almost certain that most of it was originally written long before. Jordan probably noted down what he could learn about the beginnings of the order soon after, if not even before, he became a Dominican himself towards the end of 1219; and he continued taking notes until shortly after he arrived in Bologna in 1221 as provincial of Lombardy. Then he stopped, presumably because he was too busy. This is why his narrative breaks off so abruptly. Subsequently he wrote a piece on the death of his friend, Henry, who had joined the order with him. In 1233 he did little more than add a preface and undertake a minimal revision of what he had already written.

Jordan's information about the beginnings of Dominic's life and preaching derived largely from the people he could talk to in Paris. A wider-ranging and more up-to-date attempt to extract the testimony of those who had known Dominic was made in connection with the Canonisation Process in 1233, following the solemn translation of his body. Nine Dominicans were interviewed in Bologna, including incidentally John of Spain, who is the same person as the 'John of Navarre' who features in several of the stories which follow. In addition a great many people were questioned, though in a less expansive way, in the south of France, where Dominic had begun his career as a preacher. The evidence of this two-part investigation is obviously of immense value as a source of knowledge about Dominic, but it must be borne in mind that it is evidence provided in response to official questions designed to discover Dominic's sanctity, not in order to satisfy the curiosity of would-be biographers. It is also clear that some of the brethren had rather a garbled understanding of Dominic's early history, incorrectly supposing him to have been already a canon of Osma when he was a student at Palencia and making too immediate a connection between his time in Palencia and the beginning of his public career as a preacher (155).*

After the canonisation of Dominic in 1234 it is not surprising that lives of the new saint begin to appear. The first was composed, within a few years, by a Spanish Dominican, Petrus Ferrandi. He was able to fill out the story told in Jordan's *Libellus* with some extra information, chiefly from Spain itself and from the south of France, but he did not have access to, or at least did not use, the material acquired during the Canonisation Process, nor did he undertake or benefit from any systematic quest for further anecdotes about Dominic.

* Numbers in parentheses refer to the texts translated below.

In 1245, for the first time, the order took steps deliberately to accumulate stories about Dominic: in that year the general chapter called for people who had any such stories to send them in, and thereafter several appeals of a similar kind were issued, the last being in 1314. But it was material of a particular kind that was wanted: miracles in the first place, but also other edifying tales. What is envisaged is not material for a full-dress biography, but material to support the cult of the saint and inspire the brethen.

The results of the 1245 appeal were officially passed on to Constantine of Orvieto, who was commissioned to write a new life of St Dominic for use in the liturgy, incorporating the new material. This initiates a new phase in Dominician hagiography, in which there is an increasing emphasis on the miraculous and a growing tendency to make the figure of Dominic more central, at the expense most notably of Diego, and also to make the story more edifying. Constantine arranged most of his legenda thematically rather than chronologically, according to different types of miracle, and this arrangement was preserved by Humbert of Romans in his legenda, which officially replaced that of Constantine in 1256. A consequence of this is that the public, historical context of Dominic's work disappears almost entirely from view.

In 1259 another semi-official collection of stories was published within the order, the *Lives of the Brethren*, compiled by Gerald de Frachet from material submitted in response to an appeal by the Chapter of 1256 for miracle stories and other edifying tales. A whole section of this work is devoted to Dominic.

Apart from these more or less official texts, a variety of individuals composed writings on St Dominic, all of them adding some previously unrecorded details. Thus Bartholomew of Trent, in the mid 1240s, produced two brief accounts of Dominic in his large hagiographical compilations. Stephen of Bourbon († circa 1260), who joined the order in Lyons within a year or two of St Dominic's death, included in his collection of anecdotes for the use of preachers several stories which he had heard from the brethren concerning the beginnings of the order and about Dominic's preaching in the south of France. In 1276 Rodrigo of Cerrato completed the final version of his collection of saints' lives, in which he devotes more space to Dominic than to any other. On the basis of a visit to Caleruega, Dominic's birthplace, in 1272, he was able to report a local tradition about Dominic's mother.

At much the same time, in 1278, Stephen of Salanhac abandoned work on a book *On the four things with which God has made the Order of Preachers distinguished*, which was later, after his death in 1290, edited and enlarged by the great Dominican historian, Bernard Gui, who had made profession in Salanhac's hands in 1280. Salanhac himself had been received into the order by Peter Seilhan, one of Dominic's first recruits, who retained until his death a profound devotion to Dominic and a great confidence in his prayers. Thus, through Salanhac and Gui, an oral tradition going back to the very earliest days of the order was preserved, though it must be admitted that Salanhac's chronology is sometimes rather inaccurate (e.g. in 142, where he has considerably oversimplified the circumstances of Seilhan's mission to Limoges and misdated it to the year in which Dominic first dispersed his brethren).

At some time in the 1280s Cecilia, a Dominican nun in Bologna, dictated her memories of Dominic. As a young woman, she had been the first to make profession in Dominic's hands in the new monastery of San Sisto in Rome in 1221, and before that she was privy to all that happened at Santa Maria in Tempulo before the nuns there moved to San Sisto. Unfortunately she was blessed with a highly creative imagination and some of the details in her anecdotes are patently false, and in the case of one of the miracles she reports we have many other sources for the same story which suggest that she has elaborated the event almost beyond recognition. Nevertheless, her account of Dominic's bodily appearance has been confirmed by an examination of the relics, and it is likely that, even if many of her stories are incredible as they stand, they give us a vivid and basically reliable sense of what it felt like to be in Dominic's presence. If she has distorted the events, she has probably not distorted the mood.

Later in the 1280s a friar of Erfurt, Dietrich of Apolda, undertook a full-scale life of Dominic, which he then rewrote entirely on the basis of documents received from Bologna in 1288, including the Bologna Canonisation Process and the miracles dictated by Cecilia. In the late 1290s he sent a copy of his book to the Master of the Order, Nicholas Boccasino, later Pope Benedict XI, at the latter's request; Boccasino then asked some Italian to revise it. The unknown reviser took the occasion to append a little compilation describing Dominic's ways of praying, now known as the *Nine Ways of Prayer*. This compilation almost certainly pre-existed its insertion into Dietrich's *Libellus*, but it is impossible to reconstruct it in its earlier form and to determine to what extent it was reshaped and perhaps expanded by the reviser of Dietrich.

Even in the collection of miracles put together on the orders of Berengarius (Master of the Order 1312–1317) on the basis of the appeal made at the chapter of 1314 there are several new anecdotes about things purported to have happened during Dominic's lifetime. Some of them seem to belong more to the domain of folklore than of history, but that does not mean that there is no information at all to be gleaned from these tales. It has been shown beyond doubt that some very exact historical details are found in some of the stories about St Peter Martyr compiled at the same time, referring to a period not very much later than the death of Dominic.

As we have noted, the material assembled in this rather haphazard fashion was primarily intended to be edifying or to support the cult of the saint by expanding the list of his miracles, including, of course, an ever growing catalogue of posthumous miracles. And many of the stories thus collected first appear long after the events of which they tell, which enhances the likelihood that they have grown in the telling.

However, it should not surprise us that new material could still be brought to notice even in the fourteenth century. As we have already remarked, the Dominicans were not at first attempting to collect all that could be discovered about the life of Dominic, and even when they did make a more systematic effort to assemble material, they actively sought it only among Dominicans. And of course an itinerant preacher like Dominic was just as likely (if not more likely) to be talked about by the people on whom he made an impression as a preacher, that is to say, by and large, people outside the order, as he was to be talked about by his own brethren, few of whom, in any case, had had any sustained acquaintance with him. And the very uneven response of the brethren to the successive appeals for stories suggests that, even if they did have something to report, they could not always be relied upon to take the trouble to write it down. Even in Bologna, which was supposed to be the repository for tales about Dominic, the author of the *Nine Ways* picked up two local Dominican stories about Dominic which had seemingly not been communicated to Gerald de Frachet. There is thus a whole diffuse oral tradition which, bit by bit and no doubt very incompletely, found its way into the written literature. And each item in it must be assessed in its own right to see what nuggets of genuine information it may contain, whether about factual details or, more vaguely, about the sort of impression left behind by Dominic.

The very diffuseness of this tradition has at least one inestimable advantage, even if it means that some aspects of the tales reported are more suspect than they might have been had they been collected more briskly. Explicitly or implicitly, many different witnesses are involved in the transmission of our knowledge of Dominic: we are seeing him through many different pairs of eyes. It is this diversity of vantage point, perhaps, more than anything else, which allows us patiently but confidently to build up a rounded picture of a remarkable man who, as his contemporaries attest, deeply affected those who came into contact with him.

↩ Part One ↪

INTRODUCTION

Vladimir J. Koudelka OP

❧ 1 ❧

THE FIGURE OF DOMINIC
IN ITS HISTORICAL CONTEXT

THE IMAGE OF THE SAINT

There is scarcely a saint of the Middle Ages for whose life and work we possess as many authentic sources as we do for those of St Dominic. The many surviving charters and Bulls and other such documents make it possible to determine exactly where he was, often to the precise day, and thanks to the papal letters given to him as founder we are also able to follow the ideas which he submitted in his petitions to the papal curia and which the chancery incorporated into the official Bulls. This sort of record is almost entirely lacking for Dominic's contemporary, Francis of Assisi.

In spite of our excellent sources, the historical image of Dominic was distorted soon after his death and adapted, especially by Dominicans, to suit current trends of fashion. In order to counteract the resistance within their ranks to the acceptance of unpopular functions and tasks, such as that of Inquisitor, assigned by the Roman Curia in some places to the Order of Preachers, people felt impelled to make Dominic an Inquisitor, although the papal Inquisition did not exist during his lifetime. Or they invested him with another office which did not exist at the time, that of Master of the Sacred Palace (theologian to the papal court), although such a conception of Dominic does not fit his real character at all. Thus a distorted image of him was formed, which has persisted down to our own century and been adopted by the literature of the world.

Even Dante represents Dominic as being 'gentle to his own, harsh towards his foes' (*Paradiso* XII 57).

In our own century historians have endeavoured to rediscover the authentic Dominic by means of a critical examination of the sources, and it is now possible to give a truer picture of his character. His psychological and spiritual temperament combined opposing elements, which he managed to unite in an harmonious balance. And the Order of Preachers, which he created, like his own personality, bears witness to a very distinctive character and to his rich charismatic endowment. There is nothing excessive or exaggerated in them; everything has its rightful place, everything is like the correct answer to a precise question. And there were many questions at the time when Dominic lived, each of them expressing some plight of the world and the church of the period: external threats to the West from Islam and various pagan peoples, the internal menace of false doctrines, the decline of the classical religious orders, changes in economic and social structures (the beginning of industrialisation and the growth of the cities).

HEIR TO THE PIONEERS

Even the small Castilian village of Caleruega in the diocese of Osma shows all the signs of menace, fortification and resettlement. The inhabitants of Castile had carried the chief burden of the liberation of the Iberian peninsula from Islamic domination, a struggle which had known many setbacks. When Dominic was born in Caleruega in about 1174 (the date can only be inferred approximately from his course of studies), the neighbourhood was still fresh from the resettlement which followed the expulsion of the Moors. The village with its defences, his parents Felix and Jane, well-to-do and godly people (his godmother is described as being 'of noble birth'), all these factors shaped the character of the young Dominic.

From an uncle who was an archpriest Dominic learned Latin, so that in due time he could go to Palencia to study the liberal arts and then conclude his education with the study of theology. During a severe famine which occurred while he was at Palencia he sold his precious books and founded a hospice for the poor (13, 155). As a result the way opened for his entry into the recently reformed cathedral chapter of Osma.

At Osma Dominic's chief obligations were the liturgical praise of God and contemplation. But he was torn away from his contemplative tranquillity in 1203–1206: he had to make two journeys into northern Germany as a companion of his bishop, Diego of Azebes, who had been sent on an embassy by King Alfonso VIII. They were to ask in the king's name for the hand of a noble lady for Prince Ferdinand and, since their first embassy was successful, they were sent back to escort the lady to Castile.

In the course of these two journeys Dominic met two of the perils which were threatening the West at this time: the Albigensian heresy in southern France (109) and, in Germany, the pagan nomadic tribe of the Cumans who had invaded Thuringia as auxiliaries in the army of the Bohemian king Ottokar I and ravaged the country with terrible atrocities. Impressed by the physical beauty of these fair, blue-eyed men and moved by compassion for their unbelief and by the challenge of winning them for Christ, Diego and Dominic decided to go as missionaries to the Cumans, if the pope gave his permission.

Innocent III denied permission, so Diego and Dominic set out to return to Spain (110). On the way back, however, in the spring of 1206, near Montpellier, they met the three Cistercian monks who had been entrusted by the pope with the mission to counteract heresy in the south of France. The legates were all set to throw in the sponge in desperation; their preaching and their disputes with the heretics had remained fruitless. As soon as they began to speak, the dissenters reproached them with the corruption of the clergy and the wealth of the church and pointed out, by contrast, the exemplary moral conduct of the itinerant Albigensian and Waldensian preachers. It would accordingly have been better, perhaps, to reform the clergy first and create fundamentally new forms of religious life to correspond with the newly awakened sense of the 'apostolic life' (111–115). But where was the person with the necessary time and commitment for such a task?

The encounter with the frustrated papal legates was for Dominic what the meeting with the lepers was for Francis of Assisi: it finally determined his way of life. Until now Diego and he had considered the 'apostolic life' merely in their minds; now the two men made it their own in practice. With the papal legates they began to walk from village to village, begging their sustenance, debating with Albigensians and Waldensians (116–120, 127). The newly founded monastery of nuns at Prouille, established about the end of 1206, a very poor monastery at the outset, served as their base of operations (175–177).

After the death of Bishop Diego in Osma on 30 December 1207 (122–126) and the return of the Cistercian monks to their monasteries, the enterprise virtually disintegrated. After the murder of the legate Peter of Castelnau in early 1208, when Innocent III proclaimed a crusade against the heretics and their secular protectors, everything seemed to be lost.[1]

The only one who did not lose heart was Dominic (125). During one of the most brutal religious wars in history he wandered about the most endangered areas, sought to enter into conversation even with the erring and misled, endured and suffered with the people. He was little concerned that, as a canon, he ought to have been in residence in Osma, though at the same time he could understand the Cistercian abbots withdrawing to their abbeys, as was their duty.

For more than eight years during his stay in Languedoc he grew in knowledge of God and of God's will in this torn and afflicted country (20, 54–57). He reached the conclusion that the damages, wrought over a long time by heresy (falsehood, or truth stressed one-sidedly), the outmoded structures of the church and the corruption of the clergy, could only be overcome by launching a new community, adapted to the emerging conditions in the world and to the new mentality. During his many years of activity in southern France he must have experienced how insufficient the energies of a single individual are. And the only possible remedy would be to found a new religious order.

A NEW ORDER

In Languedoc, where Dominic called himself 'the humble servant of the preaching', a small band of co-workers had joined him, but without any firm commitment to him. In April 1215, however, a few men made profession in Dominic's hands in Toulouse (130). Among them was Peter Seilhan, who gave Dominic the house in which the new community found accommodation, after Dominic had paid the debts long owed by the Seilhan family to the Jews in Toulouse. Subsequently Bishop Fulk of Toulouse, a former troubadour, father of a family and Cistercian monk, granted his approval of the foundation (131). Dominic valued this man, although they did not always share the same views – Fulk was a supporter of the crusade against the Albigensians and recruited crusaders in France and Belgium, whereas Dominic backed and promoted the 'action of faith and peace' in the true sense of the phrase.

Concern for the faith was the main focus of the new order, whose basic principles we can discover from Fulk's charter. It was an order of priests, whose members practised the imitation of the apostles in their way of life.

In the late summer of 1215 Dominic accompanied Fulk to the Fourth Lateran Council in Rome, to request confirmation of the order under the name of 'Order of Preachers'.[2] Papal confirmation was not, strictly speaking, required, because the bishops possessed the authority to found and admit new orders in their dioceses. It could, however, confer on the young order a stronger support and so make it less dependent on the person and the whims of the diocesan bishop.

The procedure for confirming a new order was for its rule

to be incorporated into a Bull of Confirmation. This is how, for example, the Carmelites and the order of St Francis were confirmed. Canon law recognised basically only three kinds of religious: hermits, monks and canons, and in addition the military orders. Among which of these was Dominic's order to be classed, when its very name proclaimed its incompatibility with all of them? The pope, on the other hand, was aware that the Council was likely to issue a canon forbidding new religious rules, thereby forbidding the setting up of new religious orders. This canon would not apply to Dominic's community, obviously, since the community was already in existence before the Council; all the same, the pope advised Dominic to choose an established rule, already recognised within the church, and he promised that he would then comply with his request.

This is the second time that Innocent III has interfered with Dominic's plans. It meant that the founder would have to do without a rule of his own – not in itself a major catastrophe. But Dominic foresaw the consequences that would attend the adoption of one of the ancient rules: it would imply belonging legally to one of the traditional orders, which would mean being forced into existing structures which would not allow him to carry out his new ideas, which were so essential to him.

Dominic returned to Toulouse in the spring of 1216 and he and his brethren chose the Rule of St Augustine, by which he had lived as a canon of Osma. They chose the Augustinian Rule, not for what it contains, but for what, by virtue of its universality, it does not contain. This enabled them to specify in the customs which they added to the rule the goal of their order and the new means for attaining their goal, without contradicting the rule.

When Dominic presented himself again in Rome in December 1216 to receive the promised fulfilment of his desires, it was already Innocent's successor, Honorius III, whom he encountered. On 22 December he received from the papal chancery, without any difficulty, a Bull confirming the existence of the community of St Romain in Toulouse and its canonical life according to the Rule of St Augustine and taking the community under papal protection. The text of the Bull, consisting of established formulae of which hundreds of copies were drawn up each year, did not need to be submitted to the pope by the chancery.

Now Dominic and his brethren were officially regarded by the universal church as members of a religious order. But there is as yet not the least sign of papal recognition of the essentially new thing for which Dominic was seeking confirmation, an Order of Preachers whose very name would indicate its purpose. For this reason Dominic continued his single-minded efforts. With his pleasant manner and his genuine poverty he won people's good will in the labyrinthine world of the curia, in which most of the papal staff were chiefly interested only in receiving 'tips'. In particular he won over the senior papal notary, William, later to become bishop of Modena and then Cardinal of Sabina (67–68). William succeeded in obtaining from the pope his friend's dearest wish, getting the final copy of the Bull of 21 January 1217 changed, as we can ascertain from the original even today, so that the epithet *praedicantes* (people who are preaching) was replaced by the substantive *praedicatores* (preachers). In this letter Pope Honorius III bid Dominic and his brethren proclaim the gospel fearlessly. Dominic had now achieved his first goal (147).

At this time Dominic was still concentrating on the diocese of Toulouse and its religious problems. He conceived the idea of having professors and students come from Paris to Toulouse to assist the friars in their task of preaching and to instruct them in theology. The pope endorsed his plan and the papal chancery presented him with the required letter to the University of Paris (166). It was not crusaders that Dominic wanted to recruit against the heresies, but professors of sacred scripture from the most famous university of the West. Had his idea materialised, it would have led to the establishment of a university in Toulouse. But Dominic never got round to sending the papal letter to Paris; instead he abruptly changed his plans.

SENT OUT INTO THE WHOLE WORLD

Dominic's two visits to Rome broadened his horizon and opened his eyes to the plight of the entire church and of the world. He realised that it was not only the south of France that was in need of preachers of the authentic Word of God and that the work of peace (*negotium pacis*) was necessary not only in areas already ravaged by war, but everywhere – the whole church was yearning for it. He also suspected that in Toulouse the power of Count Simon de Montfort, the leader of the crusaders, was not very strongly established. On 18 January 1217, the feast of the Chair of St Peter, the two princes of the apostles appeared to him in St Peter's, giving him the mission, 'Go and preach'. In a vision he saw his breathren going into the whole world two by two, preaching the Word of God (91).[3]

Hardly had he returned to Toulouse when, in August 1217, he sent out the few friars he had. Neither the protests of Simon de Montfort and Bishop Fulk nor the objections of his own brethren were able to alter his resolve (87–88). When Raymund, Count of Toulouse, reconquered the city on 13 September, the friars were already on their way. Seven of them went to Paris (167), where they were to make the order known and where some of them were to study theology in the university. Two friars sent to Spain were unable to achieve much, not least because of the opposition of the hierarchy, well known for its distrust and rejection of new orders.

The sending out of the friars marks a new phase for the small, but already international, order (international in the sense that we find several nationalities represented among the first brethren). Dominic abandoned their attachment to the diocese of Toulouse, at the same time attempting, though very cautiously, to break loose from the Augustinian branch of religious life. For the time being the Rule of St Augustine, the name 'canon' and the title of 'abbot' for the superior of the community were retained, disguising the newness of the order from a mistrustful hierarchy.

From the beginning of 1218 Dominic was once again in the Eternal City. Now his chief concern was to receive recognition from the pope for the universality of his order and for its special charism, worldwide preaching springing from an apostolic way of life. On 11 February Honorius III granted to the order the authority to preach anywhere in the world and he named the new community the 'Order of Preachers', as though the 13th canon of Lateran IV calling a halt to the rise of new orders had already lapsed.

Even in Rome Dominic never forgot that he was a preacher and an apostle. He lodged in an almshouse, probably near the Lateran. Apart from preaching in the churches of Rome, his solicitude reached out to the poorest among the Roman women, the recluses. Immured at the entrances to the basilicas and in the Aurelian wall, they barely managed to survive in impossible hygienic conditions, without any spiritual care being taken of them (179–180). Dominic's most significant work on behalf of the women of Rome, however, was the reform of the Roman nuns. Innocent III, in his renewal of the whole church, had not lost sight of the reform of his own diocese. In 1207 he decided to reform the six convents of women within the city walls and to build a new convent for the sixty or so nuns in order to make monastic discipline and religious life possible for them. The convent was to be erected near the old basilica of San Sisto. He entrusted the project to the English order of the Gilbertines, who specialised in the care of convents of women. The Gilbertines, unfortunately, never took up the papal project and after the death of Innocent III the construction of the new convent at San Sisto was suspended. Precisely at this moment, in 1218, while Dominic was in Rome, the project was taken up again and Dominic himself was charged with its realisation.[4] He got in touch with the individual convents in order to win them over for the reform.

In the summer of 1218 Dominic left Rome and returned to his own country of Spain after an absence of thirteen years. His friars were at last able to get a firm foothold in Madrid, where a convent of women also came into being (178). By way of Toulouse Dominic then went to Paris, where he arrived in May 1219. Here he found about thirty friars from different countries, many of whom were former students and professors from the university of Paris. There were patrons who were enthusiastically supporting the new order, but there were also adversaries worried about their own revenues and prestige. That is one reason why the friars were not allowed to conduct public services or to preach in their own chapel. On a small scale the conflict was already being played out which was to erupt in Paris some decades later between the secular clergy and the mendicants.

In the summer Dominic arrived in Bologna, another famous university town, and he found a strong community there; as in Paris, students and professors from the university had been entering the order. The soul of the community was Reginald of Orleans, former dean of the collegiate church of St Aignan and professor of canon law, who had penetrated deeply in a very short time into the spirit of Dominic and his order. Also in Bologna Dominic made the acquaintance of Diana d'Andalò, the daughter of a rich and powerful family, who fell for the ideal of following Christ and made profession in Dominic's hands, although there was as yet no convent of women in Bologna in the care of the Order of Preachers (184).

In November Dominic was at the papal curia in Viterbo, where he especially discussed the difficulties of the friars in Paris. Honorius III intervened on their behalf. The representatives of the Gilbertines happened to be at the curia at the same time, and they formally renounced their proposed role in the reform of the Roman nuns. It was at this time that the founder of the Order of Preachers was officially given responsibility for seeing the establishment of a reformed monastery at San Sisto through to its completion.

Among the Roman nuns, however, Dominic encountered little enthusiasm. Only five out of the six sisters in the financially ruined monastery of Santa Maria in Tempulo seemed ready – and not without some opposition – to be reformed (182–183). Of the other convents only isolated sisters allowed themselves to be won over.

While the building of San Sisto advanced under the supervision of a few Friars Preachers, Dominic departed for Bologna. There, in May 1220, the first general chapter of the new order, which was to give the order its legal constitution, took place.

THE CONSTITUTION OF THE ORDER OF PREACHERS

A decree of Lateran IV required that all orders of monks and canons were to hold a general chapter every three years. Dominic, however, adopted the Cistercian practice, preferring that the general chapter should be held annually. The period of transition and of concessions, during which he had had to move very cautiously in order to disguise the newness of his order for fear of its being confused with the lay orders which the bishops frowned on, was now definitely over. The order was firmly established; almost no one was questioning its necessity any longer and it had the complete support of the pope. It was time now for the order to replace the inadequate constitutions it had in its initial period and to give itself new constitutions to clarify its identity. What had been lived so far must now be expressed in precise and accurate language by experts in canon law. Such experts were not lacking in the community – there was Paul of Hungary, for instance, and Moneta of Cremona. And so there arose what has been called a 'cathedral of constitutional law', which is even today acclaimed as a 'masterpiece of human thought' (Léo Moulin). In the Canonisation Process the friars refer to these constitutions as 'the rule of Brother Dominic'.

In 1220 the order renounced fixed incomes and revenues. Not only the preachers on their travels, not only the individual friars, that is, but their communities too were henceforth to live off alms. Other constitutions were composed or revised on study, prayer, preaching, asceticism and the common life, and they all had but a single aim: the training and formation of a good friar and a good preacher, who would live faithfully according to the gospel and proclaim the whole gospel, without curtailment. The organisation of the order likewise received new structures, essentially different from those of the old orders. So, despite the adoption of the Rule of St Augustine, something truly new had arisen in the church, a new order.

THE LAST YEARS OF THE SAINT'S LIFE

After the end of the general chapter Dominic undertook a long missionary journey through northern Italy.[5] Here the situation was, if anything, even more embroiled than in the south of France: struggles between the adherents of the pope and those of the emperor, rivalries between noblemen and townspeople, conflicts between the upper and lower classes in the cities. Often these clashes had religious overtones. Lombardy too was infected by Albigensianism, which had, moreover, split into several distinct sects. Dominic realised again how little he could accomplish alone or with but a handful of assistants. He therefore endeavoured to found priories of the order in the main urban centres or to make preparations for such foundations. Later on this policy was proved to have been the only right one. Dominic was, as it were, sowing seed; only later would its rich harvest become visible.

In addition, he himself sensed that his physical powers were beginning to diminish.

In December 1220 he again appears in Rome.[6] A whole range of problems and concerns were in need of answers. Thanks to the personal effort of Honorius III a settlement was finally reached between the parish of St Benedict and the Dominican priory of St Jacques in Paris, so that at last the Friars Preachers could accomplish their mission publicly and independently. Their relationship with the university was also developing. At the suggestion of Dominic, the pope sent a whole series of letters of thanks to the university of Paris, as well as to different cities and monasteries, thanking them for the support they had given to the Order of Preachers. The pope's words convey the impression that favours shown to the Friars Preachers were favours done to him personally. In these documents a particularly fine trait of the saint's character is revealed: his gratitude.

During his stay in Rome in the winter of 1220–1221 his greatest concern was for the completion of the reform of the nuns of Rome. The construction of the new monastery was nearing completion. The friars had been living for some time in a separate building there, so a double monastery was coming into existence, as at Prouille. Because the sisters were to live in strict enclosure, the friars had to assume responsibility for administering their material goods as well as for their spiritual welfare.

Dominic composed a special rule for San Sisto, consisting of a compilation from the Rule of Sempringham, the constitutions of the Cistercian nuns and other constitutions; it is known as the Rule of San Sisto. After San Sisto later adopted the constitutions of the Friars Preachers, the Rule of San Sisto continued to exist in the order of the Penitents of Mary Magdalen, which gained a foothold especially in Germany.

On 28 February 1221 Dominic transferred the five sisters from Santa Maria in Tempulo and some sisters from Santa Bibbiana and other convents to the new building and established the enclosure there. The commission of three cardinals, including Cardinal Ugolino, which had stood by him during his efforts for the reform, was also present. In April Dominic's friend Bishop Fulk brought a few sisters from Prouille with him to Rome, to be a support to the rather haphazardly thrown together community of San Sisto and to introduce it to the religious life.

During the night after the installation of the nuns Dominic moved the ancient picture of the Mother of God, probably the oldest surviving Byzantine icon, from Santa Maria in Tempulo to San Sisto.[7]

Dominic did not succeed in reforming all the Roman convents of women (who would be capable of that?), but the influence of the reformed monastery of San Sisto was so powerful that in the Rome of the thirteenth century new convents of women emerged, patterned after the model of San Sisto, and the old ones allowed themselves to be renewed along similar lines. So Dominic's work of reform became normative for the future.

The pope assigned to the friars the ancient basilica of Santa Sabina on the Aventine Hill, which had formerly belonged to the family estate of the Savelli, from whose lineage Honorius III was descended.

For the last time Dominic left the Eternal City. In May the second general chapter was held in Bologna. While the first one was principally a legislative chapter, the second one concerned itself above all with the organisation and expansion of the order. Only four years had passed since the sending out of the friars from Toulouse, but already there were twenty-five priories in various countries. More friars were waiting in Bologna to be sent to their native lands, England, Scandinavia, Poland and Hungary. Dominic had never lost his desire to convert the Cumans and now his brethren were to go to Hungary with the mandate to press on to these nomads and preach Christ to them. Another group was to go to the centre of the dualist heresy, to the Bogomils in Bosnia, from where, again and again, new emissaries of heresy had penetrated to the West. It was the task of the Scandinavian friars to keep track of the missionary work among the pagan peoples of eastern Europe.

In order to facilitate the order's administrative and apostolic work, the chapter divided the order into territorial units, called 'provinces'.[8] Provinces were organised even in areas which up to now could boast of only one priory or even none at all. This far-seeing optimism of the friars is amazing, an optimism which certainly arose from genuine hope.

After the general chapter Dominic continued his strenuous mission of the previous year in northern Italy. At last, ill and exhausted, he trudged through the most intense heat to Bologna, where he arrived at the end of July. He did not even have a cell of his own or a second habit. There he died on 6 August 1221 (30, 59–61).

Cardinal Ugolino, the papal legate, who was staying in Bologna at the time, attended the funeral with his entourage of bishops and abbots (65). That Ugolino himself was the main celebrant at the funeral rites was not so much intended to enhance the splendour of the celebration as to express his close friendship with Dominic, which had arisen during their faithful collaboration in the interests of the church of that time. It was Ugolino again who, as Pope Gregory IX, canonised Dominic at Rieti on 3 July 1234.

✑ 2 ✑

CONTROVERSIES
OVER THE APOSTOLIC LIFE

THE SOURCE OF ST DOMINIC'S SPIRITUALITY

The external history of a saint and a religious founder tells us very little about his inner spiritual development and, specifically, how he interpreted his existence in the light of the Word of God and how, once touched by that Word, he translated it into action; in short, his spirituality. The Word of God, however, does not fall on virgin soil in anyone, it encounters natural dispositions and an inherited temperament.

This process is described so graphically in the texts contained in the first section, below, that we should not water them down (1–68). The traits which are clearly visible in the character of the man Dominic are constantly being called by God's demands and by his Word into new ways of conduct and new responses, which he offers to God first of all in his prayer and contemplation. The texts in the second section, concerning Dominic's prayer life and his contemplative attitude, are so numerous and convincing that readers can get for themselves a clear idea of Dominic as a man of contemplation (69–103). It was under the influence of these texts that Fra Angelico painted the saint in the cells of San Marco in Florence always in a meditative posture, with his gaze fixed unceasingly on Christ and the mysteries of salvation.

His natural power of empathy and his compassion not only gave Dominic a more profound experience of faith in prayer and meditation, they also awoke in him a sense of responsibility for the church and for the world of his time. In him we see verified something which is attested over and over again in the history of the church: once people have attained a certain degree of contemplation, they feel compelled to enter into the tensions and aspirations of their age and to grapple with its needs and its ills on the basis of their contemplative vision. We observe this in Bernard of Clairvaux or Teresa of Avila, who frequently left their monks and nuns behind in their seclusion, while they themselves worked untiringly, without any damage to their contemplation. It even seems that the contemplative life of these people was nourished by their very struggle with harsh and troubled human situations, which thereby became opportunities for new encounters with God, in which new experience of the good news of Jesus Christ could be gained; such experience has a religious character, even if it does arise out of a particular cultural, economic and social milieu and is coloured by it and by the concept of humanity current at the time.

Dominic was impelled to action not only by the specific needs of church and world, but also by a sense of accountability in face of the gifts of grace entrusted to him. Although we know about these charisms of St Dominic, they are not as easy for us to grasp as his external activities or the order which he founded. He left behind him no theory of the spiritual life, which would permit us to study his spirituality and fit it into a system and reduce it to clear concepts. In this age of computers and systematisation we run the risk of searching for a system of clear concepts even in spirituality and of forgetting human nature in the process.

To trace Dominic's Christianity, as lived by him, we have only his work and his activities in the world to go on. Historically we know both very well; in both he gave the entire church new spiritual impulses, which probably contributed more to her inner development than any theoretical treatises on the spiritual life would have done. Like every Christian, every saint, every charismatic, Dominic was shaped by the spiritual climate of his time, without which we are unable to understand him and his mentality, his actions and his way of life. The climate of his time was dominated by the ideal of 'the apostolic life' or 'imitation of the apostles'. Of Dominic himself Pope Gregory IX said, 'I knew him to be a man who imitated completely the life of the apostles.' This is the key to the spiritual personality of Dominic and to the understanding of his achievement.

THE AMBIGUITY OF 'THE APOSTOLIC LIFE'

At the end of the twelfth century and the beginning of the thirteenth, religious thought was dominated by the concept of 'the apostolic life'. This idea was not new, but in this period it fascinated whole crowds of people.

Its historical development passed through several phases, with the result that the appeal to 'the apostolic life' was ambiguous and even controversial. For centuries the monks had claimed the apostolic life for themselves: like the first Christians they 'devoted themselves to the apostles' teaching and fellowship, to the breaking of bread and to prayer' (Acts 2:42). They were 'of one heart and soul and no one said that any of the things he possessed was his own' (Acts 4:32). Faithful to the example of the apostle Paul they earned their livelihood with the work of their hands.

In the eleventh century the canons regular became the monks' rivals. Pope Gregory VII, and indeed his predecessor before him, rallied the people to oppose simoniacal and morally corrupt clergy. This movement of reform received its arsenal of ideas and slogans from Peter Damian († 1072): return to the primitive church, life according to the gospel and the model of the apostles, including poverty – these were to become the norm for the life of the clergy and especially the canons, these were to constitute the source for their piety. The canons discovered the ideal of common life in poverty, in line with the Rule of St Augustine. And another element was added: preaching. Like the disciples of Christ, the followers of the apostles were also sent out to preach the gospel. As a result of this development, a conflict arose between monks and canons over which of them was leading the more authentic 'apostolic life', though at the same time they were both united in a common struggle against the secular clergy who did indeed preach and administer the sacraments, but could not display the moral character of the apostles.

The imitation of the apostles involved preaching by word and example (*verbo et exemplo*) and demanded accordingly a life consistent with the word that was preached. *Verbo et exemplo* became almost a battle-cry and had the effect of dynamite. The crusaders brought from the Holy Land, together with alleged relics of the passion of Christ, a deepened devotion to the incarnate Saviour and a vivid picture of Jesus, the poor preacher, which captivated broad sections of the populace. This piety stood in opposition to the opulence of the large abbeys, with their extensive landed property, and to the cathedral chapters, with their rich endowments, and to the way of life of the secular clergy, who were effectively retainers of their feudal lords. The money economy, commerce and the beginnings of industrialisation were having the effect of making the rich ever richer, especially in the cities, while the poor became ever poorer and more deeply in debt. In response, countless Christians made their own the desire for some model with which they could identify themselves, and they found such a model most clearly in the picture of the poor and suffering Christ and his apostles. Voluntary poverty became the manifesto of several itinerant preachers, evoking a response among large sections of the population. In this way a new hallmark of the apostolic life was added to 'word and example': itinerancy, being on the road like Christ and his apostles. And the message proclaimed by the itinerant preachers was often one of criticism of ecclesiastical authority or a call to people to oppose simoniacal and bad-living clergy. This led to some sharp conflicts with the hierarchy.

The men who adopted this way of life were enthusiasts, such

as Robert of Arbrissel († 1116) in western France, Norbert
of Xanten († 1134) in northern France and Germany, Fulk of
Neuilly († 1201) in the region round Paris, and many others.
With them itinerant preaching was preceded by a period spent
as a hermit, as with Francis of Assisi soon afterwards, who
passed the years 1206–1208 in solitude before taking up itinerant preaching. In time these wandering preachers settled
down and established communities and religious orders for the
men and women who followed them.

There were other itinerant preachers too, whose one-sided
perception of the apostolic life led to their downfall. They
identified its perfection exclusively in terms of voluntary
poverty and itinerancy, and regarded these as automatically
entitling people to be preachers and sometimes even to administer the sacraments, with no need for any mandate (*missio*)
from the church. As an example we may notice Tanchelm (†
1115), who had great success among the people of Flanders,
Peter of Bruys († 1126) and Henry 'of Lausanne' († after 1145).
They broke with the official church, which refused to give them
a mandate to preach.

The best known of these extremists is Waldes, a rich mer-
chant from Lyons, who appears first in about 1175. He urged
the people to imitate the apostles in poverty. He himself lived
off alms, and he lashed out against the sins of the clergy and
demanded a return to the primitive church. When he was
forbidden to preach the faith, he disregarded the prohibition
and so became a schismatic.

In due course, at the turn of the twelfth and thirteenth
centuries, the paths of these more or less schismatic preachers
crossed, especially in the south of France and in Lombardy,
with those of yet another group of itinerant preachers and
their followers (among whom women were represented in great
numbers): the so-called Cathars or Albigensians. Their rigorous
asceticism, of a Manichean temper, refusing all contact with
the flesh and the world (in which they saw only the domain of
Satan's power), their nomadic life and their poverty made a

profound impression on the people. Their excellent organisation, their provision of a relatively easy hope of salvation for the ordinary believer, together with a demanding programme of austerity for the 'perfects', and the support of the feudal lords secured for the Albigensians a rapid expansion. For the bulk of the faithful it was not their dualistic speculation about a good and an evil God which was decisive; people's minds were captivated by the Cathars' moral and religious earnestness.

This phenomenon is not confined to this epoch. Historians can observe the same sort of thing in other eras too. In Dominic's time literary culture and higher education were reserved to the clergy and were practically inaccessible to the laity; the laity, however, felt engaged by religious ideas and values in proportion to the extent to which the message proclaimed was authenticated by the life of the preacher. The great respect and admiration which the itinerant preachers earned among the masses was due to their poverty, often linked with begging, and by their ceaseless wandering. The people saw in these things the credentials of the apostolic life, as it was presented in Luke 9:1–6, to which the preachers appealed; they also took them as constituting the yardstick of moral perfection. This is certainly not the first time in the history of the church that certain tenets of the bible were overstressed at the expense of others, giving the impression that there is but a single approach to the kingdom of God. It is usually the great idealists and zealots who, in times of crisis in the church or religious life, allow themselves to be seduced into such exclusiveness. But the one-sided emphasis on some ideals puts an undue strain on people's physical and moral limitations and so leads to tensions, and its failure to consider the different personal gifts of different individuals means that it contains within itself the seeds of disunity.

Whereas the modern mentality sees poverty as a socio-economic problem, for the adherents of the poverty movement it was a religious, theological and even an eschatological preoccupation, as the researches of M. Mollat have shown. Poverty was seen as the path to salvation. All those who were actually poor, whether of necessity or by their own free choice, and also the sick and widows and orphans found themselves on this path. In this way they were like Christ, especially if it meant that they had to endure persecution, contempt and rejection. In the light of salvation history and redemption through Jesus Christ, temporal goods were seen not as belonging to people, but as being loaned to them and put at their disposal for them to use. The giving of alms was consequently the duty of the rich and to demand alms was the right of the poor. The rich man was only giving back what had been entrusted to him when he gave alms, and he was at the same time atoning for his sins. The itinerant preachers spread this view among the people and the people took it up avidly; and they observed that there was a considerable discrepancy between the ideal and the actual lives, especially of the clergy. What was at stake was not just speaking about poverty as a means of proclaiming the gospel: the unity of word and deed, of preaching poverty and living in poverty among the poor, became a goal in itself. Of course only an élite could translate this high ideal into a reality, so there was a real danger, more in practice than in theory, that the faithful would come to be divided into two categories, the 'perfects' and the second-class believers, as was the case with the Cathars.

BLIND ALLEY

In the time of St Dominic, then, the religious climate was rather heated. The bishops were perplexed and powerless in face of the poverty movement, nor could an adequate response be expected from the institutional church, whose pastoral care was mainly concentrated on the administration of the sacraments, to the neglect of doctrinal preaching, and whose clergy were often ignorant and leading far from exemplary lives. Nor could the monks do any better; their abbeys and monasteries were enmeshed in the feudal system and the responsibilities that went with their large estates. The catholic itinerant preachers confined their followers, both men and women, in monasteries, thereby excluding them from the kind of life they themselves, for longer or shorter periods, had led. So by and large the field was abandoned to the heretical and schismatic itinerant preachers.

The religious founders of the eleventh and twelfth centuries, most of them former itinerant preachers, chose the traditional forms of religious life in order to escape from a whole range of conflicts which seemed insoluble to them. They wanted from the outset to spare their followers the opposition they had themselves experienced. They certainly felt justified in their criticism of the deplorable state of the church of the time and in particular their criticism of the hierarchy and the clergy; but hanging over them the whole time, like the sword of Damocles, was the risk that they would have their mandate to preach withdrawn by the hierarchy, as happened to Robert of Arbrissel. In any case the traditional forms of religious life seemed most appropriate to them as a way of dealing with the real or presumed abuses of the itinerant life among the motley array of their followers.

There was another problem too which caused some tension. Possessing nothing was a presupposition of the apostolic life and of itinerant preaching. So were they to live by the work of their hands or by begging? If they were priests and wanted to live as mendicants, there was a canonical obstacle in their way: priests were forbidden to beg by canon law, in case the real poor were deprived of their sustenance. But if they chose to live by the work of their hands, they would have no time for preaching and travelling.

Again, the followers of the wandering preachers were for the most part laypeople, who were forbidden to preach the faith. But where was the dividing line between proclaiming the faith on the one hand and exhorting people to penance and to the mortification of vice on the other? The catholic wandering preachers ordinarily did not possess any great theological education and the laymen in their ranks lacked it altogether. When and how could this deficiency be remedied in order to confront the heretical itinerant preachers, as far as possible, with a solid knowledge of sacred scripture?

With the foundation of monasteries the wandering preachers got caught in the rigid machinery of canonical regulations, which knew only three forms of religious life, those of the monk, the canon and the hermit. All three depended on stability, on staying in one place, which was incompatible with travelling round and preaching. And mendicancy had to be given up as well, because of the feudalistic thinking of the time, for which a community without real estate was inconceivable. But on the other hand preaching in poverty, according to the ideal of the apostolic life, demanded insecurity and without it was liable to lose its credibility.

Faithful to the traditional practice, the former itinerant preachers established yet more monasteries in remote places, apart from the surging life of their time; they continued to abandon the cities to the heretical and schismatic preachers.

As a result the apostolic life, the fruit of the reform movements of the previous centuries, found itself stripped of the means and weapons which the reform had made available to it. The institutional structures in the church proved stronger than the enthusiasm of a few, charismatically endowed individuals. Divisive forces in society and in the church seized the means we have been considering and used them against the church, without needing to worry about established forms and structures.

It would, however, be wrong to say that the entire hierarchy reacted with incomprehension to the heretical movements of the time. There were individual prelates, regional councils and popes who assessed the situation correctly and endeavoured to take remedial measures. Foremost among them was Pope Innocent III, with whom Dominic had to deal in the early stages of the foundation of his order.

INNOCENT III'S INTERVENTION

Innocent III (pope 1198–1216), a man at the height of papal power, met the religious movements of his time with understanding. He was genuinely interested in the reform of the whole church; he saw in the poverty movement of the period a possibility for the renewal of the church, and he hoped to safeguard its unity by incorporating this movement into the church.

The pope was himself stirred by its spirit. In February 1207, when the new manner of preaching in Languedoc was in full swing, he laid aside the precious purple robes and furs with their gold and silver trimmings, which recalled the splendour of the Byzantine emperors, and put on 'religious' dress, that is, an ordinary woollen garment with sheepskin instead of furs. Since that time the white colour of their attire has remained a distinctive mark of the bishops of Rome. It is not improbable that the pope's gesture was influenced by the report of his legates in the south of France, in which they described the new style of preaching and requested his authorisation for it. In the Bull of appointment on 31 May 1204 issued to Arnaud, abbot of Cîteaux, he was still charging him to take action against the heretics with the assistance of the secular authorities and to punish them with expulsion, excommunication and seizure of their assets. But in his reply of 17 November 1206 to the legates' report he agreed to the new, peaceable action against the heretics and gave his envoys advice of a quite different timbre. He advised them to look for reliable men whose lives would display Christ's poverty to the poor and who would not be afraid of going about in degrading clothes, men of ardent spirit, ready to go out to people who were generally despised. They were to go to the heretics and turn them from their error by means of their own exemplary behaviour and discourse (127). At the very least, the relative chronology of these events makes one wonder!

Innocent III's outward gesture of changing his attire corresponded to the deep inner conviction revealed in his work *On the wretchedness of the human condition.* The pope had the courage to see in the religious lay movements of his era not only a danger, but a contribution to the building up of the church as well; and he tried to make use of it. In 1201 he succeeded in winning back for the church a large number of the Humiliati in Lombardy and in fashioning a new order out of their married and unmarried men and women. Similarly, when Durandus of Huesca, a Waldensian leader, abandoned the sect in 1207 after the debate at Pamiers, in which Bishop Diego and Dominic took part, Innocent III reconciled him and his followers with the church and gave them a suitable structure, with the result that the order of the Poor Catholics came into being. Soon afterwards there came the reconciliation of Bernard Prim and his followers, another Waldensian splinter group, known as the Poor Lombards. At the same time, the pope extended extraordinary benevolence towards Francis of Assisi and his first followers.

Despite his generosity, however, Innocent had little success with his new orders. The reason for the failure lay primarily in the orders themselves. They clung too stubbornly to their old practices and did not give up provoking the bishops with their criticism and reproaches. The hierarchy, on the other hand, remained suspicious of them, because they came from the ranks of the schismatics and preached as laypeople. In spite of the pope's support, in spite of his letters of recommendation and his admonitions to the bishops, neither the Poor Catholics nor the Poor Lombards were able to survive. The quick decline of the former is particularly remarkable, since they had experienced an extraordinary expansion in a very short time in Italy, France and Spain. Most bishops lacked the magnanimity and patience of Innocent III. Dominic must have experienced at close range the progressive breakdown of the Poor Catholics and the difficulties of Durandus of Huesca, with whom he was acquainted, before he began the founding of his own order. All this certainly weighed heavily on him and his work. The 13th canon of the impending Lateran Council, which would prohibit the establishment of new religious orders, was already in the air.

DOMINIC'S APOSTOLIC LIFE

THE RISK OF THE NEW FOUNDATION

It was a great risk, in the circumstances of the time, to contemplate founding a new order which was on the surface so strongly reminiscent of the religious communities which had come to grief. Would Dominic's keen mind and prudent judgement, his charismatic gifts and his ability to make friends be sufficient to avoid all the pitfalls? That Dominic ventured it at all was due to the strength of his faith. At first only the essential principles of what his order was meant to accomplish were clear to him. Subsequently he had to learn to accept defeat, to make compromises, to be guided anew by concrete situations, to listen to unexpected promptings of the Spirit, until his work, the first apostolic religious order, could finally mature.

It is fascinating to observe how, step by step, Dominic turned his basic ideas into a reality, despite great difficulties. One of these basic ideas, the notion of the apostolic life, was not his own invention; he took it over and lived it in his own way. Countless people were inspired by it at the time, but they all stressed different aspects of it, and most of the attempts made to practise it failed, just like numerous foundations of orders and monasteries which had come into existence in great abundance in the twelfth and early thirteenth centuries. Dominic placed his own emphasis quite differently from his contemporary, Francis of Assisi, for instance. Although the fundamental elements of the apostolic life were the same for all – preaching, combined with travelling about and begging, to which some people added study of the scriptures and common life – the problem lay in harmonising these elements.

Dominic kept a firm grip on this point, slowly feeling his way ahead.

How did he ultimately succeed in reconciling the various elements, encumbered as they were by differing traditions from the past, as well as by the experiences of Dominic's own time? We see a distinct development in Dominic over the years, in which two important stages are the formation of the order in the context of a single diocese and, secondly, the transformation of this diocesan order into a worldwide order.

FROM DIOCESAN TO WORLDWIDE ORDER

The first attempt to harmonise some of the elements which had for a long time been considered incompatible is known to us from the charter of June or July 1215, in which Bishop Fulk of Toulouse approved the way of life of Dominic and his brethren (131). They received from him a mandate to preach in his diocese, and since they were priests their mandate was specifically to preach the truths of the faith (the 'rule of faith', *regula fidei*); in this they obviously differ from the heretical and schismatic itinerant preachers, but also from the Poor Catholics, the Catholic Lombards and the fraternity of Francis of Assisi, which were associations made up largely of laypeople and so were allowed only to preach penance and to give moral exhortations. Moral preaching was part of the task of Dominic's preachers in Toulouse too, in addition to doctrinal preaching; but they were also appointed to root out heresy, and it was this that the bishop placed at the head of the list because, from a chronological point of view, this constituted the reason why the new order had come into existence.

Their manner of preaching was quite new for priests. Of course some priests had occasionally adopted such a manner before, but there was no order of priests which practised it as such. Their preaching did not take place in a church – after all, the brethren in Toulouse did not possess a church. It did not involve any territorially defined pastoral responsibility (*cura animarum*); their business was the salvation of everyone and must be pursued, therefore, wherever people were suffering from problems of faith or morals or religious ignorance. Accordingly the preachers had to travel in order to reach the people who were in need and not wait for the people to come to them. Fulk's charter expresses the point in two words: *religiose incedere*, that is, travelling as religious and in community, in the sense that they were to travel two by two. Monks, canons and hermits were religious who *lived* a religious life (*religiose viventes*), meaning that they lived by a rule and, generally, in community; Dominic's brethren were to go further and live a religious life on the road, they were to be mobile religious. This meant abandoning local stability and the security that went with it in a patriarchal community. It meant being at the mercy of the hardships of the road and the uncertainty of finding accommodation and sustenance.

At first Dominic's community confined itself to two bases, Prouille and Toulouse. Neither centre was a 'monastery' in any current sense of the word. As the liturgy could not be celebrated without a church, the brethren took part in the liturgy in the nearest church and, when they were on the road, they attended the services that were available wherever they found themselves at the time. Because the communities comprised only a small number of brethren and the friars were often away on preaching trips, one can compare their bases with the hospices of the Cathars or the Waldensian schools, in which leaders were educated and wandering preachers found shelter in case of illness or when they needed to recover from fatigue. The first Franciscans went even further and dispensed entirely with fixed accommodation and contented themselves with chance lodging for the night; they were not permitted even to regard their hermitages as being their own property.

The programme of the new order in Toulouse corresponded largely to the intentions of Innocent III set forth in the Bull of 19 April 1213 convoking the Fourth Lateran Council. The pope declared the main task of the forthcoming council, after the recovery of the Holy Land, to be the reform of the whole church, and he spelled this out in terms of a list of objectives: eradicating vices and implanting virtues, correcting abuses, moral reform, strengthening the faith, settling disputes and establishing peace, putting an end to oppression and fostering liberty. It looks as if Fulk's charter of 1215 for the diocesan preachers under Dominic contains verbal echoes of the papal Bull. At any rate the pope's objectives and those of Dominic in the religious domain are essentially the same.

Fulk, together with Dominic and his diocesan order, was also anticipating the 10th canon of the Council, which recognised that the bishops were often prevented from fulfilling their office of preaching and might even lack the necessary learning for it, and accordingly directed them to entrust the preaching of the Word of God to qualified men in their diocese.

Another of Dominic's goals for his brethren, that they should have a solid theological formation, was also picked up by the Council, in the 11th canon, obliging the bishops and superiors of collegiate churches to employ salaried teachers to instruct the clergy at least in secular learning, and requiring that regular theological schools should be established in metropolitan churches.

If Innocent III, just before the Council, refused to give his approval to Dominic's order, the reason was not that he disagreed with the ideas embodied in the order. On the contrary. But the pope had misgivings that the new order might run into opposition from the bishops, as had happened to the other new foundations he had approved, and might be destroyed thereby. That is why he advised that the new order should adopt an established rule.[1]

In itself, the adoption of an established rule would have led inevitably to the same results as in the case of the earlier catholic wandering preachers: it would have meant a commitment to stability (and so the end of itinerant preaching) and the acceptance of property. Innocent III did indeed promise that, after the adoption of an established rule, he would give

Dominic the confirmation he wanted of everything else, but what did this really mean? Through their choice of the Rule of St Augustine the preachers of Toulouse joined the great family of Augustinian canons. The Rule as such consists only of generalities and would not compromise Dominic's design in the slightest, but the customs and observances of the canons were a different matter, leaving no room for daring innovations.

Dominic, however, was not the man to allow himself to be easily discouraged. He made concessions at first, while at the same time working patiently for the realisation of his original plan, and the plan itself took on a new character after the order was transformed into a worldwide order.

ITINERANT PREACHING (132–150)

Dominic did not in any way reduce his basic idea of preaching, and in time he prevailed completely. In his Bull of 21 January 1217 Honorius III officially gave Dominic's brethren the title of 'preachers', and barely two years after the Council's ban on new orders the pope spoke quite matter-of-factly of 'the Order of Preachers' (11 February 1218), as though such an order had always existed.

As the order expanded geographically, beginning with the sending out of the brethren in the summer of 1217, the content of its preaching also expanded. In the diocese of Toulouse the ministry of the Word by Dominic and his brethren was principally directed towards the controversy with heresy, and this remained true of the two houses of Prouille and Toulouse. But in Paris or Bologna the brethren had to adjust more to the classical mode of preaching customary in university towns. Rather than refutation of heresy, the proclamation of the truth of the faith as a whole came to the fore. Soon the evangelisation of heathens was added, as we can see in Honorius III's Bull of 6 May 1221 to the Danish king, Waldemar II, in favour of the Friars Preachers.

What is most astonishing of all, though, is the number of

privileges showered upon the Order of Preachers by the pope. Tradition, canon law and church doctrine all assigned the pastoral office to the bishops; it consisted above all in the authoritative preaching of the Word of God, in official explanations of moral doctrine and in the power to admonish and punish. The assistants the bishops were to choose, according to the decree of Lateran IV, to help them in their preaching, were naturally entirely dependent on the bishops. But now, with the Order of Preachers, both the tradition of centuries and canon 10 of Lateran IV lost their stranglehold. The pope entrusted the preaching mandate directly to a religious order, as such, without giving any role to the bishops and without any regard for diocesan boundaries. The result, as M. H. Vicaire says, was a radical transformation in the conditions of evangelisation. Now, in addition to the bishops, the priories of the Friars Preachers also had the right to give a mandate to preach to any of their members who were competent. These preachers were expected to pay their respects to the local bishop, when they entered his diocese, and they were to ask his advice, but nothing more.

It is extraordinary that an order with a mandate originally reserved to the bishops was capable of holding its ground and of being accepted by the bishops and clergy, while the Poor Catholics, for example, disappeared. What was the reason? In the first place, the Friars Preachers were priests. And secondly, the Rule of St Augustine cast a protective veil over the newness of the order. Nor did they present themselves as competing with the bishops, but as their co-workers. Most bishops were aware of their inability to meet the demands of the ministry of the Word of God, and they recognised the impossibility of finding among their own clergy men suited to this ministry. So the preachers sent by the pope were welcome, especially as they took on the task of preaching free of charge.

As evidence and proof of their papal mandate the friars carried the so-called Bulls of Commendation with them. More than thirty copies of these papal Bulls are preserved to this day, scattered all over Europe from Sicily to northern Germany, from Spain to Poland (149). By contrast with Francis of Assisi, who even in his Testament forbade the Friars Minor to ask for letters from the Roman curia 'for a church or for any foundation or under the pretext of preaching or because they are being persecuted in their own bodies', the particular objective of the Dominican Order required recommendation and support from the bishop of Rome.

In his letters of commendation Honorius III defines ever more emphatically the distinct mandate of the Friars Preachers to accomplish in voluntary poverty the work of proclaiming the gospel, to explain the truths of the faith and to preach the Good News with complete dedication. He impressed upon the bishops how useful, in fact how indispensable, the preaching office of the friars was for the church. Divine providence had raised up this order as a new force against the abundant wickedness of the world and made it a remedy for the wounds of the church. The whole world was the field in which the Friars Preachers sowed the Word of God.

Behind words like these there stands no frivolous flatterer, but a man of hope who believed in God's love for the world and the church. The Order of Preachers at this time comprised only a small handful of men, most of them still in formation. But Honorius did not even hesitate, because of their insufficient number, to thrust aside all legal norms and, for example, attach to Dominic six monks from different monasteries who, under his direction, were to preach an important mission in northern Italy. It was already contrary to tradition to send monks out as preachers; to subordinate them, in addition, to a barely known superior of an absolutely new order constituted an unprecedented novelty (148).

The fact that the new order was accepted by the hierarchy and its 'interference' in the pastoral office of the bishops tolerated without strong resistance is due, no doubt, to the exemplary life of the friars. Officially they were, of course, known as canons, which was a concession made by Dominic; but instead

35

of appearing like dignitaries, as was normal for canons, Dominic insisted on unpretentiousness. That meant, first of all, travelling on foot instead of riding on horseback. Dominic himself was an indefatigable walker (28, 143) – a calculation of the distances he covered after the foundation of the order gives us an average of forty to fifty kilometres a day (about twenty-five to thirty miles). Had the traveller of that time not been exposed to perils scarcely known today, roaming through largely virgin scenery might have been an elevating experience. But the most troublesome aspect of this way of life was spending the night in hospices for poor pilgrims, teeming with fleas, lice and bugs, to such an extent that the friars were often unable to sleep a wink. We hear of young friars who even wanted to leave the order because they could no longer put up with the hardships of such a way of life.

The strain and unpleasantness involved in itinerant preaching became for the Friars Preachers, though to a much greater extent, what manual labour was for the monks: it was their penance. Pope Honorius III admonished them repeatedly to accept this penitential manner of life as a way of atoning for their sins, and, to encourage them, he granted them an indulgence for it. Although the friars, with their incorporation into the canons' branch of religious life and their acceptance of churches, became more settled and stable than they were as a small band of preachers belonging to a diocesan order, they did not abandon itinerant preaching. Dominic knew how to blend conventual life with itinerant preaching in such a way that no contradiction arose and that living in priories, with a commitment to regular celebration of the Divine Office, did not work against mobility.

POVERTY AS A SOURCE OF MOBILITY (151–163)

The driving force of the friars' mobility as wandering preachers in Dominic's community was poverty. In this, a distinct line of development from the diocesan order to the worldwide order can be noted. According to Fulk's charter the diocesan preachers of 1215 are to travel about 'in evangelical poverty', a clear reference to the poverty of Christ's disciples when they were sent out (Luke 10:1–20). It was part of this kind of poverty to travel on foot without money. Dominic had been practising this apostolic way of life since 1206, two years earlier than Francis of Assisi. During the years of the 'holy preaching' in Languedoc he depended chiefly on the alms he obtained by begging. He also received help for his livelihood from the nuns at Prouille.

In 1215 he mitigated poverty in one respect: his order in Toulouse accepted some material support from the diocese. The bishop granted Dominic and his companions one half of the portion of the tithes of the diocese which was allocated to the poor. Fulk justified this grant by saying that it was only right and just to give material support to the preachers who, for the sake of Christ, had chosen evangelical poverty, and this was in line with apostolic tradition (1 Cor. 9:1–14). This support, however, remained limited to the barest essentials; it is expressly mentioned that the preachers will be cared for in the case of illness and when they need to rest, and they are to receive food and clothing, but at the end of the year the unused balance was to be returned to the diocese.

This is all vastly different from the older orders. These were obliged to assist the poor out of their own possessions. Now, by contrast, a new order was arising on the basis of evangelical poverty and its members, being poor themselves, depended on the assistance of others. They depended on it because, as priests, they were not supposed to beg and they were, moreover, so occupied with their job that they were unable to earn their living by working with their hands. The Poor Catholics did not do manual labour either, but the Humiliati and the Lombards attached great importance to it. Francis of Assisi similarly required his brethren to earn their living ordinarily by their own labour and to live off alms only in exceptional circumstances. For Francis poverty was above all an essential part of following the poor Christ; it went with being despised and persecuted and humiliated. Only secondarily, for Francis, was poverty the foundation for a convincing preaching of penance and for living an exemplary life. In Dominic's case the deepest roots of evangelical poverty lie in the notion of the apostolic life. It is required of the apostle that he renounce every kind of security and this in turn becomes the source of his independence, freedom and mobility. It is not a question of renunciation for renunciation's sake; it is rather a matter of evangelical humility, which is not an ascetic means, but an essential ingredient in the exemplary life modelled on that of the apostles.

A new stage begins with the adoption of the Rule of St Augustine by Dominic's order. The brethren decided at the same time 'that they would not own properties, to ensure that no worldly responsibilities and worries would hinder their task of preaching; they would only accept revenues with which to provide for the food they needed' (Jordan of Saxony). To obtain papal confirmation, the foundation in Toulouse had to have some possessions; no other material basis for the existence of an order of priests was known at the time. But all the same Dominic insisted on mendicancy for his friars when they were travelling, in line with his own constant practice.

As the example of John of Navarre shows (160), conflicts could arise between the existing legal status of the friars and the larger aims of the founder. When John was sent to Paris, he asked for travelling money to which he, as a canon, was entitled. Dominic could not persuade him to forgo this right in favour of mendicancy. He finally gave him the money for the trip, but at the same time he gave him a talking to which he never forgot for the rest of his life.

Even before the general chapter of 1220 the priories disposed of their fixed revenues. The general chapter then decided to base the maintenance of the Friars Preachers entirely on mendicancy. Without worrying about canonical regulations, an order of priests was thus established on the basis of something which up to then had been forbidden to priests (162).

Dominic saw mendicancy in the context of the apostolic life. To beg for alms was the apostle's privilege. 'If we have sowed spiritual seed for you, is it too much if we reap material things from you?' (1 Cor. 9:11). In this sense, asking for alms is not begging – it is an exchange. The preacher gives people the Word of God and receives from them in return the necessities of life. In his Bulls of Commendation Honorius III stressed the apostolic character of the preachers' voluntary poverty. Combined with their constant travelling, it gave them interior and exterior freedom. Unencumbered by responsibility for the administration of property and independent of the power-structures of this world, the Friars Preachers could proclaim the gospel much more freely.

As an integral part of the apostolic life, poverty contributed to the living example of the preacher and of the renunciation he had made for the sake of the gospel, a renunciation which, as the pope noted, also included being despised. It was there-fore an essential element in the asceticism of the apostolic life. What the earlier catholic wandering preachers had failed to accomplish, a combination of individual personal poverty with common conventual poverty, Dominic ingeniously achieved. Not only were the preachers to supply their wants by begging as they travelled about, but, from May 1220 onwards, their communities were to do so as well. Every morning two friars left the priory in order to beg in the streets and from door to door, so that the brethren in the community could have susten-ance for one day. That the friars sent out to beg sometimes returned without having received anything and the brethren in the community had to go hungry directed them even more strongly towards the vocation of the poor. In faith they aban-doned themselves to providence, which occasionally helped them miraculously (102).

Another reason why the priories of the Order of Preachers depended on mendicancy was their abandonment of manual labour, from whose proceeds monks had traditionally provided both for themselves and for the needy. In the new order study had replaced manual work. Friars pursuing their studies were unable to earn their keep and the itinerant preachers were not allowed to accept pecuniary offerings to support the friars living in the priory.

STUDY AS SPIRITUAL WORK IN THE SERVICE OF PREACHING (164–173)

In connection with the obligation of religious to practise manual labour, the monks and some orders of canons appealed to St Paul (2 Thess. 3:10). The Humiliati and Francis of Assisi likewise could not envisage a way of life without manual labour. The Waldensians, on the other hand, and in some circumstances the Cathars regarded it as a hindrance to effective preaching; the Waldensians took Jesus' words, 'Do not work for the food which perishes, but for that which lasts unto eternal life' (John 6:27), as being sufficient to exclude manual labour. With Dominic there is no trace of manual labour. From the outset he introduced study in its place, as an indispensable means to every apostolic activity and to greater fecundity in the contemplative life. His love of books was generally known. Already during the 'holy preaching' in Languedoc he and his fellow-workers had books with them, a veritable luxury at the time. They forsook much that might have seemed necessary, but not books. According to Jordan of Saxony, the grant made to the order by the diocese of Toulouse in the early period was meant to be used, among other things, for the purchase of books, but this was a concession to the requirement that the clerical brethren should say the Divine Office; in the case of Dominic's preachers their need of books was more extensive, and Dominic had no hesitation in recognising it.

Even so, Dominic was always ready to give up his cherished books for the sake of a higher love. As a student in Palencia he sold his books to help the needy. And at the end of his life he confessed that he had learned more from the book of charity than from any other book. In him books did not outweigh charity. But he had had to learn from bitter experience the consequences, for the church of the time, of the theological ignorance of the clergy, who could administer sacraments all right, but were unable to preach the Word of God. Pope Innocent IV († 1254), for example, had to content himself with requiring of poor priests simply that they should know the truths of the faith contained in the Creed (which is what laypeople were obliged to know in any case), and that they should believe in Christ's presence in the Eucharist and be capable of dispensing the sacraments and celebrating Mass. This last they could learn from any priest. Bishops, in addition, had to be able to answer questions regarding the faith, if necessary with the assistance of some more knowledgeable person. By contrast, the heretical movements of the time, in their own way, stressed to excess the ministry of preaching and neglected the sacraments.

Dominic responded to the educational needs of the church, as well as to the need for preaching. His first friars were certainly far less educated than he was. It is safe to assume that their educational level was equivalent to that of most of the simple clergy. But Dominic saw to it that they had the chance to improve their education and he inspired them with an eagerness to study theology and sacred scripture. In Toulouse he sent them to the English theologian, Alexander Stavensby, who was lecturing in the cathedral school (165).

The study of sacred scripture ranked equally high among the Cathars and the Waldensians; their preachers were educated in their hospices and schools. The same was true of the Poor Catholics and the Catholic Lombards. For the latter two orders, however, study was principally directed towards controversy with the heretics. Francis of Assisi, for his part, regarded with suspicion the attempts of some of his brethren to introduce study into his order, even though he recognised the need for some theological training for the preaching of penance.

Dominic, on the other hand, insisted quite consciously on a thorough theological formation for his friars. In his eyes study with a view to preaching, which in turn was to contribute to the salvation of other people, was indispensable as a component of the apostolic life in the full sense of the word.

The fourth Lateran Council upheld the importance of study for preaching, just as Dominic did. Accordingly, early in 1217, Dominic formed a plan to get professors and students of theology from Paris to come to Toulouse, so that they could train the preachers and assist them in the proclamation and defence of the faith. However he soon abandoned that plan; instead he sent his friars to Paris and Bologna, the two centres of ecclesiastical learning. In the long run, of course, the order could not send all its friars to Paris or Bologna for their education, but in the meantime the number of teachers and students who joined the order at both universities increased so greatly that the theological formation of the brethren could increasingly be secured in every house that the order established.

The general chapters of 1220 and 1221 enacted a series of regulations governing study and formation in the Order of Preachers. They show what importance study had acquired in the young community – another unique phenomenon in the history of religious life. Even novices were to be encouraged to handle books carefully, and they were to be told to be always reading something or going over in their minds what they had previously read, by day and by night, in the cloister and on the road, and they were to memorise as much as possible. Students were to be supervised by a specially appointed friar, who was to assist them in their studies. The more talented students could be assigned cells of their own so that they could stay up at night to study without being disturbed and without disturbing the others. Every community had to have a teacher of theology, whose lectures the members of the community were obliged to attend. In this way the continuing education of all the friars was assured. The bishops at the fourth Lateran Council had not even dreamed of such a possibility.

The highest goal of study in the Order of Preachers was the spiritual welfare of others; but the student who applied himself seriously to the study of scripture and theology derived the greatest benefit himself as well, for his own prayer life and contemplation. Study enriched his spiritual life and supplied him with material for his inner vision, so that he would not lose himself in subjective imaginings and unrestrained sentimentalism.

The importance of study in the life of the order is underlined by several constitutional provisions. The Divine Office was to be celebrated briskly to make more time for study. And every superior was given authority to dispense his subjects from any conventual obligations which were likely to interfere with study, preaching or the good of souls. Study, we notice, is ranked equally with preaching and the good of souls as a reason for dispensations. The responsible use of dispensations by the superior was not meant to be a concession to human weakness; it was an appropriate way of facilitating the order's pursuit of its proper objective in any situation in which different values were tending to encroach upon each other. Dispensations were a matter of achieving the order's goal in the best possible way.

Responsible bishops soon understood what advantages a priory of Friars Preachers could offer in their diocese for the intellectual improvement of the diocesan clergy. This is clearly expressed, for instance, in the letter of Bishop Conrad of Metz, 22 April 1221 (150).

THE NOVEL ORGANISATION OF THE ORDER OF PREACHERS

By comparison with the traditional religious communities, the new purpose of the Order of Preachers and the partly new or newly orientated means that it adopted called for new structures and a different kind of organisation. In the classical orders the various abbeys and monasteries were independent of each other. An order consisted of a union of independent abbeys or monasteries, whose inhabitants had committed themselves to their specific house. In the Order of Preachers the friars bound themselves by the vow of obedience, not to a definite priory or church, but directly to the Master of the Order. This conferred great mobility upon its whole international community and enabled the superior to assign each friar wherever the needs of the order demanded at the time. Chapters, including representatives elected from the ranks, kept a constant check on superiors to ensure that centralisation would not take control and that superiors would not become independent autocrats. The highest governing body in the order was the general chapter, not the Master of the Order. Originally a general chapter was held every year, and it possessed legislative power over the entire order. It could make changes, great or small, in the constitutions and adapt them at any time to new circumstances and needs, saving only the order's purpose and the essential means serving that purpose. In the case of disputes between provinces, priories or individuals it also possessed supreme judicial power. In addition it could discharge all superiors, not excepting the Master of the Order, so that superiors did not hold office for life, but only as long as they enjoyed the confidence of the brethren. While the general chapters of the Cistercians, which were the model for similar institutions in other orders of monks and canons, were intended to enforce a uniform discipline in all their abbeys and, where necessary, to revive such discipline, with the chapters of the Friars Preachers the age of democracy broke in on religious life. The new constitutional system received some essential impulses from contemporary secular law, in particular the constitutions of the cities of northern Italy, in which the *podestà* was also appointed by election and for a limited term of office. For the duration of the general or provincial chapter the assembly as a whole elected a group of four friars, called 'diffinitors', to whom full authority was transferred, including that of investigating and deposing superiors. Outside the time of the chapter, superiors functioned primarily as visitators of provinces and priories, to give new impetus to the various substructures of the order and to keep its spirit alive. Through the system of chapters many friars had the possibility of participating in the administration of the order as a whole or of its provinces and priories, and of taking a share in responsibility for it.

St Dominic's contemporaries reacted with some bewilderment to the novelty of his religious foundation. For example Boncompagno of Siena, professor of rhetoric at Bologna, commented that the Friars Preachers seemed to be trying to plough with an ox and an ass together (cf. Deut. 22:10), because their order was a mixture of the way of life of the monks and that of the canons. Nevertheless he pays them an oustanding tribute: 'They live on earth like the apostles, because by the word of their preaching they build up many people for salvation, especially as they preach nothing which they do not try to put into practice themselves.' If Dominic succeeded in creating a unity of word and deed in harmonising the preaching of truth with a life lived in accordance with the truth, and in fashioning an enduring synthesis out of the various elements of the apostolic life, it is in large measure due to his own balanced way of proceeding and his own personal equilibrium.

ᘦ 4 ᘒ

A MAN OF SYNTHESIS

The harmonious balance which Dominic achieved in the development of his personality amid the challenges of his age and which he, after years of resolute exploration of various possibilities, succeeded in imprinting on the Order of Preachers before he died, can be seen under several headings.

BALANCE BETWEEN CONTEMPLATION AND ACTION

In spite of the tensions between contemplation and apostolic commitment Dominic succeeded in blending these two essential elements into a unified life without any discontinuities or conflict. For him the Word of God was primary. He heard it and lost himself in it utterly in meditation. But precisely in this way it became for him a source of preaching and action. It was in attentiveness to the divine Word that he uttered his own word and shaped his own work. So his prayer became apostolic and his action took on a contemplative dimension, because it never made him turn his gaze away from God. He made himself holy in contemplation so that he could make others holy, and in making others holy he became holy himself. By 'making holy' we mean the turning towards the integrity, steadfastness and fidelity of God, which God himself brings about.

For Dominic the following of the apostles was accomplished not so much by external imitation or by activity, but above all by an interior disposition. Like Christ and the apostles who did not wish to neglect the Word of God in order to serve tables (Acts 6:2), Dominic divided his time between prayer and preaching, even if he had only the night left for prayer. It was in prayer that his words matured and it was with the help of prayer that he made his decisions and engaged his whole being in the service of the gospel and of his fellow mortals.

The tension between contemplation and action pervades the history of the Order of Preachers. The order did not actually disintegrate, as some other orders did which were unable to avoid repeatedly splitting up, but it was often tested to breaking point by the tension between the two poles. After the order began to have churches of its own, with the corresponding obligation to choral Office, Dominic managed to balance this with personal prayer. He loved the liturgical prayer of the church, but he reduced its importance, because the purpose of his order differed from that of the traditional orders. Following his example, the friars adopted the custom of quiet personal prayers (*orationes secretae*) especially after Matins.

BALANCE BETWEEN THE ORDER'S GOAL AND ITS ADOPTED MEANS

The goal of the order being new in the history of religious life, the means adopted in view of this goal had to be new too – study, for example – or else traditional means had to be transformed and given, to some extent, a new content to facilitate the achievement of the goal. Study, poverty, common life, the vows, ascetic practices, all took on a twofold character: on the one hand they contributed to the formation of a morally healthy personality and of religious who would be faithful to their calling, and on the other hand they were given an apostolic orientation, because everything was done with a view to the apostolic mission to other people. While separation from the world was the outstanding feature of monastic life, and the most important thing for the monks was their own personal sanctification, the Friars Preachers were called to service in the world. Hence their priories, as a general rule, were built in the cities and not in seclusion. In spite of the establishment of priories, which made for a certain local stability, Dominic managed to make the existence of priories compatible with the itinerant life of preaching. The community sent out friars to preach, but these friars would from time to time return to their community to find there the refuge they needed in which to recuperate their physical and spiritual strength.

Because poverty was not regarded as a value in itself, but as a means to the apostolate, the friars were allowed to own priories, churches and books, although this meant that they did have a kind of 'capital investment'. But it was not just 'dead capital', serving only to produce wealth; on the contrary, this very 'investment' compelled the friars to beg even for their sustenance. Dominic overcame the old contradiction between the mendicancy of the itinerant preachers and the supposed need to have an adequate financial basis for the foundation of priories by daring to make his priories also dependent on alms, though only certain friars were charged with the task of begging so that community life would not be jeopardised.

BALANCE BETWEEN TRADITION AND INNOVATION

In place of a rigid, unchangeable rule, the proper legal framework of the Order of Preachers was made up of constitutions, and the general chapter had the power to change these, except with regard to the order's goal and the means to that goal. This gave the community the continual possibility of daring innovations and of reforming itself without causing divisions; it also enabled the friars to adapt their activity to the changing circumstances and needs of the church and the world. Thanks to the order's unchanging purpose and the constancy of its essential means, it did not lose the values of tradition; but its enduring efficacy was ensured precisely by the constant process of renewal. Both at the level of grass-roots and at the level of the order's government everyone was equally engaged in this process.

THE WORKING TOGETHER OF AUTHORITY
AND CHARISM

Almost immediately after the decree of Lateran IV prohibiting the foundation of new orders, a new order arose in the church, without anyone at the time really noticing it. This fact is partly attributable to St Dominic's shrewdness; he was flexible enough to make allowances and still pursue his goal tenaciously and unwaveringly. Had Dominic been an unimaginative legalist with a purely legalistic turn of mind, it would never have occurred to him to contravene the canon of an ecumenical council. Nor would he have ventured to bypass so many legal norms and engrained traditions in such a short period of time – for example, the exclusive rights of the bishops and their delegates in the matter of preaching, the ban on priests begging, the requirement that monasteries should have property – and to introduce instead practically the opposite. He could only do so, without bringing about self-destructive conflicts with laws and traditions, because he was charismatic. He believed in the transforming power of the Spirit, free from any false respect for petrified institutions and antiquated norms, which had become ends in themselves and were blocking access to the message of Christ. Endowed with the gifts of the Spirit, he possessed also the courage to be humble, which inspired him not to appropriate his gifts to himself, but to use them for the good of the community and to submit them to the scrutiny of ecclesiastical authority. The history of the church reveals many instances of the fact that it is precisely from the tension and the working together of personal charism and church authority that genuine and fruitful results are obtained.

Dominic, fortunately, encountered in his opposite numbers in the hierarchy, not just sticklers for principles, but men who were pastors of souls and who took their commission, their charism of service, seriously. Honorius III, himself an advocate of the apostolic life, valued the ministry of preaching highly and, as we can see from his sermons, he appealed constantly for the unity of word and example, It was this same pope who made light of the legal barriers which were likely to obstruct Dominic's work; without abolishing them officially, he created new legal formulations to correspond with Dominic's ideas and to further the order he had founded. He showed personal concern for this foundation, as though he himself were its author. In the collection of documents concerning St Dominic we are struck by the great number of letters from Honorius III, a testimony to the close collaboration between authority and charism. The papal chancery also contributed its bit, circumventing in its turn numerous rules and regulations, as we can see to this day in various original documents. We find corrections made to a fair copy, we find simplifications of form, which were contrary to the rules of the chancery but saved Dominic both time and expense.

Dominic's relationship with Ugolino, the most influential cardinal of his time and the protector of the Friars Minor, certainly goes back to the days of the fourth Lateran Council. It became stronger with each of Dominic's visits to the papal curia, so that the mutual respect of the two men increased and a genuine friendship developed.

So, in the circle of the bishop of Rome, Dominic met not only bureaucrats but also zealous pastors, who were passionately engaged with the concerns of the kingdom of God and the church. Thanks to their understanding and assistance he was able to overcome the conflicts and blind alleys of the apostolic life movement and to harmonise the different elements which made up such a life and to create a unique and enduring synthesis.

THE NEW ORDER'S INFLUENCE

As frequently happens with rigorous prohibitions which are merely a reaction against an abuse, the ban of Lateran IV on new orders could not restrict the work of the Spirit and prevent the emergence of something which was to be a blessing to the entire church. Dominic did not directly violate canon 13, which obliged all new foundations to adopt an existing rule and approved statues; he chose the Rule of St Augustine and adopted, in part, the statutes of the Praemonstratensians. In the orders of monks and canons their statutes served to unify discipline and to fill out the rule with detailed regulations, and they were therefore changeable and adaptable. And, in addition to the disciplinary regulations adopted from the Praemonstratensians, he was able to add statutes of an essentially new kind, expressing the novelty of his order's purpose, without actually contradicting the rule.

The introduction of statutes in the religious orders had already resulted in a certain downgrading of the various rules and had enhanced the importance of the changeable regulations. Dominic speeded up this development, so that in the future rules were seen simply as laying the foundation for religious life and as obliging religious to the three vows, but not as entailing more detailed obligations. This was how Innocent IV explained it to St Clare, for instance, when he subjected her to the Rule of St Benedict.

This development was not confined to the rise of a single order; it led to a whole new class of religious communities, the so-called mendicant orders. The Carmelites, originally an eremitical order, adapted themselves to this new type of order in 1245, as did the Augustinian Hermits in 1256. The Servites made considerable use of the constitutions of the Order of Preachers in drawing up their own statutes, and the Roman curia organised even the Friars Minor after the pattern of the Preachers. To some extent this happened under the very eyes of St Francis, who was pained by it, though he nevertheless remained faithful to ecclesiastical authority – that is his greatness.

The activity of the Order of Preachers and orders akin to it released among the rank and file of the people an hitherto unheard of enthusiasm for the faith and an unexpected zeal for the life of penance. The people had at last found those followers of the apostles who could proclaim the gospel in word and deed.

The popularity of the new apostles is demonstrated, among other things, by the immense churches of the mendicant orders all over Europe. The common people undertook the hard labour of building them as a form of religious service, the aristocracy furnished the building materials without charge, and everyone wanted to be associated with these orders and sought spiritual care from them. The level of lived faith rose quickly among people and clergy. The study of sacred scripture and theology received a splendid impetus, giving new substance and depth to people's spiritual life. Heresies found the carpet pulled from under their feet, because they could flourish best when the organism of the church was weakened by a virus in its own body. It was not direct action against them – the Inquisition would, as a matter of fact, have been unnecessary – but the enhancement and renewal of spiritual vigour in the church that brought about the rapid disappearance of false doctrines. Such was the abundance of inspiration radiating out from St Dominic. He did not only 'touch the heart of his century' (H. D. Lacordaire); through his order his apostolic spirituality is a blessing to the generations that came after him.

～ Part Two ～

TEXTS

೭ 5 ೨

THE PERSONALITY OF DOMINIC

No one, and especially no saint, is a lifeless model. As a man, Dominic was endowed with an unmistakable personality which we are able to grasp easily from several contemporary accounts. Grace did not render his temperament insipid, it clarified and strengthened it. What strikes us in his psychological disposition is the combination of delicacy of feeling and strength of will. Opposition did not discourage his uncompromising character, but his tenacious staying power was coupled with intelligence. Thus he knew how to pursue unswervingly the essential goals of his mission without exhausting his energy in fighting superficial obstacles. To his sensitivity Dominic owed an extraordinary capacity to perceive and to feel things.

He was easily moved by joy and by sorrow. He experienced both with equal depth, but sorrow did not crush him, nor did joy make him arrogant. Inner joy created in him a state of serenity, while sorrow found release in healing tears. An emotional balance developed without dulling his impressions or impoverishing his sensitivity. Heartfelt compassion opened his eyes to the needs of individuals and society. He observed how things hung together and interacted in different situations in order to call forth liberating energies in himself and in others. This is how Dominic was so capable of comforting his fellow human beings. He helped them to get to the bottom of reality, to clarify problems, and gave them in this way strength and confidence, from which they could draw hope. He himself lived by this same hope and built his work on it, and awakening hope in others was a specially good way for him to put love of neighbour into practice. That is the hallmark of all great reformers.

The evenness of his temperament was not something Dominic simply possessed from birth: he acquired it by working on himself. Although it was conditioned by the religious culture of the period, his asceticism was never morose or grim. The abnegations which he freely took upon himself served rather to develop a refined, mature personality. They were meant to free him from the dark aspects of his humanity and thus promote charity, from which sprung his indefatigable labour. The deepest roots of his gift for compassion lay, however, in God's merciful love. Dominic knew that he was someone redeemed by divine love. That realisation filled him with serenity and enlarged his heart, so that he was able to give to others the redeeming love of God.

HIS CHARACTER IN GENERAL

(1) Dominic was of middling height and slender build. His face was beautiful and slightly ruddy, and his hair and beard were reddish. He had beautiful eyes. A kind of radiance shone from his forehead and between his eyebrows, which drew everyone to venerate and love him. He always appeared cheerful and happy, except when he was moved by compassion for any trouble which was afflicting his neighbour. He had long, beautiful hands, and a powerful, beautiful, resonant voice. He was not bald anywhere, but had a complete ring of hair round his tonsure, flecked with a little grey. [Cecilia 15]

(2) He spent four years in sacred studies, and throughout the whole period his eagerness to imbibe the streams of sacred scripture was so intense and so unremitting that he spent whole nights almost without sleep, so untiring was his desire to learn; and the truth which his ears received he stored away in the deepest recesses of his mind and guarded in his retentive memory. His natural abilities made it easy for him to take things in, and he watered all that he learned with devout feelings and brought forth fruit in the form of saving works. The verdict of Truth himself pronounces him blessed: as he said in the gospel, 'Blessed are those who hear the word of God and keep it' (Luke 11:28). There are two ways of keeping the word of God: one is to retain the word in our memories,

once we have heard it; the other is to put it into practice and display it in action. There is no doubt that the second way is better, just as it is better to keep seed by planting it in the earth than by hoarding it in a box. Now this fortunate servant of God, Dominic, was adept at keeping God's word in both ways: his memory was a kind of barn for God, filled to overflowing with crops of every kind (Ps. 143:13), and his external behaviour and actions broadcast publicly the treasure that lay hidden in his holy breast. Because he accepted the Lord's commandments so warmly, and because his will welcomed the voice of his Lover with such loyalty and pleasure, the God of all knowledge gave him an increase of grace, so that he became capable of receiving more than the milk of beginners and was able to penetrate the mysteries of difficult theological questons with the humble understanding of his heart and to swallow easily enough the testing promotion to more solid food.

[Jordan, *Libellus* 7]

(3) He was of a good disposition from the time he was a baby, and his remarkable childhood promised that great things could be expected from him when he grew up. He did not join in the games of others or associate himself with those who walk frivolously (Tobit 3:17); like quiet Jacob, he avoided the wanderings of Esau, preferring to remain in the lap of his mother, the church, and the homely tents of sanctity and repose. Looking at him, you would have said that he was young and old at once; his lack of years proclaimed him a child, but the maturity of his way of life and the stability of his character were more suggestive of old age. He spurned the enticements of a dissolute world, to walk in the way of innocence. To the end of his life he preserved the glory of virginity intact for the Lord, who loves purity. [Ibid. 8]

(4) [When he had become a canon], he at once became conspicuous like a solitary star among his fellow canons. He was the lowliest of them all in his humility of heart, but he was their

leader in holiness. For all of them he was a fragrance of life
leading them on to life (2 Cor. 2:16), like incense on a summer's
day (Ecclus. 50:8). The brethren were amazed that he attained
such an unusual height of religious perfection so quickly and
they appointed him subprior, so that his superior position
would attract everybody's attention and they would all be
drawn by his example. Like a fruitful olive tree, like a cypress
which rears itself up to heaven (Ecclus. 50:11), he haunted the
church by day and by night, devoting himself ceaselessly to
prayer (1 Thess. 5:17). Claiming for himself the leisure for
contemplation, he hardly ever showed himself outside the con-
fines of the monastery. God had given him a special grace to
weep for sinners, for the distressed, for the afflicted; he bore
their troubles in the inmost shrine of his compassion, and the
warm sympathy he felt for them in his heart spilled over in
the tears which flowed from his eyes.

[Ibid. 12]

(5)   It was his very frequent practice to spend the night at his
prayers, praying to his Father with his door shut (Matt. 6:6).
During these prayers he sometimes felt such groaning in his
heart that he could not stop himself from bursting out loudly,
so that even at a distance people could hear him roaring and
crying. He had a special petition which he often made, that
God would grant him true charity, which would be effective in
caring for and obtaining the salvation of other people; he
thought he would only really be a member of Christ's Body
when he could spend himself utterly with all his strength in
winning souls, just as the Lord Jesus, the Saviour of us all, gave
himself up entirely for our salvation. He read and loved a book
[by Cassian] entitled *Conferences of the Fathers*, which deals
with the vices and with the whole matter of spiritual perfection,
and in it he strove to explore the ways of salvation and to
follow them with all the powers of his mind. With the help of
grace, this book brought him to the highest purity of conscience

and to considerable enlightenment in contemplation and to a veritable peak of perfection. [Ibid. 13]

(6)   Far more impressive and splendid than all his miracles were the exceptional integrity of his character and the extraordinary energy of divine zeal which carried him along; these proved beyond all doubt that he was a vessel of honour and grace, adorned with every kind of precious stone (Ecclus. 50:10). His mind was always steady and calm, except when he was stirred by a feeling of compassion and mercy; and, since a happy heart makes for a cheerful face (Prov. 15:13), the tranquil composure of the inner man was revealed outwardly by the kindliness and cheerfulness of his expression. In every reasonable purpose which his mind conceived, in accordance with God's will, he maintained such constancy that he hardly ever, if ever, consented to change any plan which he had formulated with due deliberation. And though, as has been said, his face was always radiant with a cheerfulness which revealed the good conscience he bore within him, the light of his face never fell to the ground (Job 29:24) [by descending to frivolity]. By his cheerfulness he easily won the love of everybody. Without difficulty he found his way into people's hearts as soon as they saw him. [Ibid. 103–104]

(7)   Wherever he went, whether he was on the road with his companions or in some house with his host and the rest of the household, or among important people and rulers and prelates, he always overflowed with inspiring words. He had an abundant supply of edifying stories, with which to turn people's minds to the love of Christ or to contempt for the world. Everywhere, in word and in deed, he showed himself to be a man of the gospel. [Ibid. 104]

(8)   During the daytime nobody was more sociable and happy with his brethren or his companions, but at night nobody was more thoroughly dedicated to keeping vigil and to prayer. Tears

waited for him at night, but joy in the morning (Ps. 29:6). The day he gave to his neighbours, the night he gave to God, knowing that by day the Lord sends his mercy and by night he gives songs of praise (Ps. 41:9). He used to weep plenteously and frequently, and his tears were his bread by day and by night (Ps. 41:4), by day especially when he often and indeed every day celebrated Mass, and by night especially when he kept watch in his uniquely unwearying vigils. [Ibid. 104–105]

(9)   It was his very frequent habit to spend the whole night in church, so that he hardly ever seemed to have any regular bed of his own to sleep in. He used to pray and keep vigil at night to the very limit of what he could force his frail body to endure. When at last weariness overtook him and his spirit succumbed, so that he had to sleep for a while, he rested briefly before the altar or absolutely anywhere, sometimes even leaning his head against a stone like the patriarch Jacob (Gen. 28:11). But then he would soon be awake again, rallying his spirit to resume his fervent prayer. [Ibid. 106]

(10)   Everybody was enfolded in the wide embrace of his charity, and since he loved everyone, everyone loved him. He made it his own business to rejoice with those who were rejoicing and to weep with those who wept (Romans 12:15). He was full of affection and gave himself utterly to caring for his neighbours and to showing sympathy for the unfortunate. Another thing which made him so attractive to everybody was his straightforwardness; there was never a hint of guile or duplicity in anything he said or did. [Ibid. 107]

(11)   He was a true lover of poverty, and he always wore cheap clothing. He confined himself to a very modest allowance of food and drink, avoiding all luxuries. He was quite content with very simple fare, so firm was his bodily self-control, and he drank wine so austerely diluted that, though it satis-

fied his bodily needs, it never blunted his fine, sensitive spirit. [Ibid. 108]

(12)   Our predecessors, who now reign with the Lord, were jealous for spiritual gifts (1 Cor. 14:12) when they lived on earth; they thought little of themselves and scorned the world. It was the kingdom they longed for, and so they were strong to endure hardship, enthusiastic for poverty, on fire with love. Surely our father Dominic, of holy memory, was one of these. While he was living with us in the flesh, he walked by the Spirit, not only not fulfilling the desires of the flesh (Gal. 5:16), but actually quenching them at the source. He displayed true poverty in his food, his clothing and his behaviour. He prayed constantly, was outstandingly compassionate, used to shed copious tears and was zealous for the good of souls. Success did not make him slack, adversity did not worry him. We could see from the works he accomplished, from his virtues and miracles, what a great man he was on earth. Now that he is with God, his greatness has been made known to us in these last days, when we were moving his holy body from its previous burial place to a more noble tomb. [Jordan, *1233 Encyclical* 2–3]

The chief characteristic of Dominic's temperament was a great sensitivity and compassion for every kind of suffering, including moral suffering, entirely in the sense of the Greek word 'sympathy' (suffering-with). He felt deeply with the poor and the suffering and this made him devote himself unselfishly to other people. But because his compassion was joined to firmness of character and genuine humility, it never seemed condescending or patronising to anyone.

(13)   While he was still a student at Palencia, there was a severe famine throughout almost the whole of Spain. He was deeply moved by the plight of the poor and resolved, in the warmth of his compassion, to do something which would both accord with the Lord's counsels and do as much as possible to remedy the needs of the poor who were dying. So he sold the

books which he possessed, although he needed them very much, together with all his furniture, and established a charitable fund. In this way, open-handed he gave to the poor (Ps. 111:9). His exemplary kindness so moved some of the other theologians and masters that they too began to give more lavish alms, seeing their own sluggish parsimony shown up by the young man's generosity. [Jordan, *Libellus* 10]

(14)   Compassion grew up with him, and indeed came forth from his mother's womb with him. As his bodily age increased, so did the work of virtue grow in him. By a kind of natural transmission he drew kindness of heart from the very heart of his mother. For she was an extremely compassionate woman. On one occasion, when her respected husband Felix, the father of St Dominic, was absent, his mother, seeing the hardships some people were suffering, gave away many of her own possessions, and then devoted to the poor a certain cask full of wine which she had, which was famous in the locality, distributing the wine amongst them. When her husband was on his way back home, as he drew near to Caleruega, his neighbours went out to meet him, and some of them insisted on telling him about the wine that had been devoted to the poor. So when he arrived home he told his wife, in the presence of his neighbours, to have some of the wine from the famous cask served up to them. She was afraid that no little embarrassment would ensue, so she went to the cellar where the cask was and knelt down and prayed to the Lord, 'Lord Jesus Christ, even if on my own account I do not deserve to have my petition heard, hear me for the sake of your servant, my son, whom I dedicated to your service.' Dominic's mother was aware of her son's holiness. Then, full of faith, she stood up and went to the cask and found it full of the very best wine. Giving thanks to the giver of all graces, she had the wine served up in abundance to her husband and the others. They were all amazed.

[Rodrigo de Cerrato 4]

(15)   Brother Ventura of Verona said that Brother Dominic was wise, perceptive, patient, kind and very merciful, very friendly, sober and fair, to such an extent that, all things considered, he did not think he had ever in his whole life seen anyone more vigorous in all the virtues, in spite of the fact that he had seen and known many good religious in various parts of the world. [Bologna Canonisation Process 5]

(16)   Brother John of Spain said that everyone found Brother Dominic approachable, rich and poor alike and Jews and pagans (of whom there are many in Spain), and he could see that he was loved by everyone, except for the heretics and enemies of the church whom he pursued and showed up in debate and in his preaching. Yet even them he lovingly urged and encouraged to do penance and return to the faith, as he himself heard and saw. [Ibid. 27]

(17)   He certainly did not lack the greatest form of charity anyone can have, the charity to lay down his life for his friends (John 15:13). Once, when he was urging one of the unbelievers, with loving encouragement, to return to the faithful embrace of mother church, the man explained that his association with the unbelievers was prompted by his worldly needs, because the heretics gave him necessary funds, which he could not obtain in any other way. Brother Dominic was so moved by sympathy that he decided immediately to offer himself for sale and relieve the poverty of this endangered soul with the price of himself. And he would really have done it, had not the Lord, whose riches are for all (Romans 10:12), made other arrangements for meeting the man's needs. [Jordan, *Libellus* 35]

(18)   A woman once complained to him that her brother was being held captive by the Saracens. He, full as he was of the spirit of pity, was stricken by a deep feeling of compassion and offered to sell himself to ransom the captive; but the Lord did not allow this to happen, since he was keeping him for a more

abundant harvest of righteousness and for the conversion of many souls. [Petrus Ferrandi 21]

(19)   Brother Frugerio of Penna said that he heard Brother Dominic's confession and from it he realised and firmly believes that he had never been tainted by any mortal sin. He also said that he was humble, kind, patient in any troubles, rejoicing in adversity, loyal, merciful, a comforter of the brethren and of others and so adorned with all virtues that, from what he saw and knew in him, he firmly believes that there was no one else like him that he had ever seen or heard of.

[Bologna Canonisation Process 48]

(20)   Abbot William Peire testified that he had never seen anyone so thoroughly humble, nor anyone so uninterested in worldly glory and all that goes with it. He also said that he accepted reproaches and abuse and insults with the utmost patience and joy, as if they were a great gift and favour. He also said that he was never upset by being persecuted; indeed, he often went his way unworried and unafraid in spite of danger, nor could he be frightened into turning aside from his path. In fact when sleep overcame him he would just throw himself down on the road or beside it and go to sleep. He also said that he surpassed all the religious he had ever seen. He also said that he utterly made light of himself and considered himself to be nothing. Also, he used to offer fatherly consolation to the sick brethren, wonderfully supporting them in their infirmities. He also said that, if he learned of anyone being in any kind of trouble, he would encourage them to be patient and give them whatever comfort he could.

[Languedoc Canonisation Process 18]

His sensitivity found expression and at the same time liberation in frequent weeping (21–26). Because he put God and his concerns before everything else, including himself, he had a keen awareness that God would not forget him. This freed him from

anxieties and constraints and allowed him to distance himself from
everything that might have oppressed him or overwhelmed him with
worry. Thus his confidence always outweighed the sense of threat or
fear, even in critical and genuinely dangerous situations. Therefore
joy always prevailed. In all privations and affronts he was conscious
of his participation in the sufferings of Christ (27–30, 54–58).

(21)   Brother Ventura said that [Dominic] used to spend the
greater part of the night in prayer and very often he spent
the whole night in church, and he used to weep a lot when he
prayed. Asked how he knew this, he replied that he very often
found him in church praying and weeping, and sometimes overcome by sleep. And, because of his long vigils the night before,
he frequently used to doze off at table.

[Bologna Canonisation Process 6]

(22)   Brother John of Spain said that he always found him
cheerful in the company of other people, but in his prayers he
used to weep frequently. [Ibid. 29]

(23)   Brother Rudolph of Faenza said that [Dominic] was very
eager and devoted and assiduous in preaching and in hearing
confessions. And he often wept while preaching and stirred his
hearers to weep. [Ibid. 33]

(24)   Brother Frugerio of Penna said that he many times heard
him saying Mass, whether in a priory or while travelling, and
on every one of these occasions he shed tears in abundance.
[Ibid. 46]

(25)   The holy father felt for the sins of others with an extraordinary compassion. When he approached any village or town
that could be seen from a distance, he used to think of all the
human misery and sin that it contained and then he would
completely dissolve in tears. [*Lives of the Brethren* II 23]

(26) He once told Brother Bertrand, his companion, not to weep for his own sins, but for those of others; this was because he noticed that he was tormenting himself excessively over his sins. His words had such a powerful effect that thereafter Brother Bertrand wept profusely for others but was unable to weep for himself, even when he wanted to. [Ibid. II 19]

(27) Brother Buonviso said that, when they needed to lodge somewhere or take a meal, [Dominic] did not follow his own wishes, but those of his brethren who were with him. And if he was badly served he looked much happier than if he was well served. Asked how he knew this, he replied that he had seen it and been present when it happened. He also said that when he was at Milan and was looking after Brother Dominic, who was ill and suffering from a fever, he did not complain about his illness, but seemed to the witness to be at prayer and contemplation. He thought this because of certain signs which he saw in his face which were generally there, when he was in good health, when he was at prayer and contemplation, as the witness knew well. He also said that, when the fever left him, then he began to speak about God with the brethren, or he would hold a book or get someone to read to him; and he praised God and rejoiced in his sickness, as he always rejoiced in all troubles, more than he did when things were going well for him. He also said that, when the witness was procurator for the brethren in the priory of Bologna and supplied the brethren in the refectory, one fast day they ran out of bread in the refectory. Then Brother Dominic signalled that bread should be put out for the brethren. The witness said to him that there was no bread there. Then Brother Dominic, with a cheerful expression on his face, raised his hands and praised the Lord and pronounced the blessing, and immediately two people came in carrying two baskets, one full of bread, the other full of dried figs, so that the brethren had more than enough. He said that he knew this because he was present at the time. He also said that he was very humble, kind, loyal and

merciful, patient, sober, zealous for poverty and for the salvation of souls and a lover of religious and of all forms of religious life. He also said that he kept the rule strictly himself, and that he did not repay evil for evil or cursing for cursing, but he blessed those who cursed (1 Pet. 3:9).

[Bologna Canonisation Process 22]

(28) He also said that when he was travelling from Rome with him, Brother Dominic used to take his shoes off whenever he left a town or village or estate and walk barefoot, carrying his shoes over his shoulder – he refused to give them to his companion, who was quite prepared to carry them – until they came near a town or village or estate, and then he put his shoes on again. When they came out again, once more he removed his shoes and went barefoot until they reached their destination. Once they came to a place where the stones were particularly sharp, and then he said to the witness, 'Here, poor wretch that I am, I was once forced to put my shoes on.' The witness asked why. Brother Dominic replied that it had been raining at the time. He also said that when he, the witness, was walking with Brother Dominic on the same journey, a downpour of water and rain overtook him, so that the rivers and streams were very swollen, and Brother Dominic, who always rejoiced in all his trials, began to praise and bless the Lord, singing 'Hail, Star of the Sea' at the top of his voice. When he had finished that hymn he began another, 'Come, recreating Spirit, come'. And he sang it loudly right through to the end. He also said that, when they came to a great expanse of water which was swollen because of the downpour and the rain, Brother Dominic made the sign of the cross over the water and told the witness, who was very nervous of the water, to go on in in the name of the Lord. Trusting in the sign of the cross which Brother Dominic had made and relying on the virtue of obedience, he went into the dangerous-looking water, and everything turned out all right. [Ibid. 21]

(29)   Brother Paul of Venice said that he never saw him angry or upset or troubled either because of the labour of travelling or because of any fierce emotion or in any other way; he saw him rejoicing in all his trials and patient when things went against him. [Ibid. 41]

(30)   Brother Ventura said that it was about the end of July, he thinks, when Brother Dominic returned from the court of the Lord Ugolino, who was at that time Bishop of Ostia and legate of the Holy See and is now the pope. The court was at Venice, he is sure. Brother Dominic returned very weary, because the weather was very hot. And although he was so tired, he spent much of the night talking about the affairs of the order with the witness, who was the new prior at the time, and with Brother Rudolph. When he himself wanted to get some sleep, he asked Brother Dominic to go and sleep too and not to get up in the night for matins; but he did not agree to this suggestion, but went into church and spent the night in prayer. In spite of this he was at matins, as the witness heard from the brethren and from Brother Dominic. After matins, the brethren told him, Brother Dominic had a headache, and from that time onwards he began to be obviously ill with the disease by which he passed to the Lord. He also said that, while he was ill like this, he refused to lie in a bed, but lay on some sacking instead. And he had the novices called to him and consoled them with gentle words and with a cheerful face, encouraging them to goodness. He endured this sickness and others too so patiently that he always seemed to be in good spirits and happy. [Ibid. 7]

Because Dominic was a man of faith, that is, because he found in faith his mainstay and also the foundation for his hope, he was able to console others and give them hope, pointing out to them new possibilities and giving them assurance. Consoling in this sense was for Dominic a practical way of loving his neighbour.

(31)   Brother Stephen of Spain said that Brother Dominic was the best possible comforter of the brethren and others in their trials. He knows this because, when he was a novice, at the beginning of his religious life, he was often subject to a variety of trials, and the advice and preaching of Brother Dominic gave him all the encouragement he needed. And the same thing happened to many other novices, as they told him.

[Ibid. 37]

(32)   Brother Rudolph said that, if [Dominic] saw a brother committing any fault, he used to pass by as if he did not see it; but later on, with a calm expression on his face, he would say to them gently, 'Brother, you have done wrong; confess your fault.' With his kind words he led them all to confess and do penance. And in spite of the humility with which he spoke he punished their faults severely, but all the same they went away encouraged. [Ibid. 32]

(33)   Brother John of Spain said that [Dominic] punished the brethren when they sinned, in accordance with the rule, but he sympathised with the sinners and was greatly distressed when he punished anyone for any fault. [Ibid. 25]

(34)   Brother Paul of Venice said that [Dominic] kept the rule strictly and perfectly himself, and he exhorted and commanded the brethren to keep it fully; offenders he punished strictly, but with such patience and such kind words that none of them was upset or disturbed by it. [Ibid. 43]

(35)   St Dominic had received into the order a fine young man called Brother Henry, a Roman citizen of very noble birth and even more noble character. When his family learned of his entry they planned to get him out again and make him return to the world. St Dominic, hearing of this, gave him some companions and sent him away from Rome to another priory. When his family heard that he was escaping they pursued him,

intending to get him out of the order. So when the novice and his companions had reached the river at a place called Ponte Quarti, near the Via Numentana, no sooner had they crossed the river than their pursuers caught up with them and were already at the river's edge. The novice saw them there and commended himself to God and to the merits of his father, St Dominic, asking the Lord to rescue him from their hands by his merits. Then a wonderful thing happened, done by him who alone works wonders (Ps. 135:4). As soon as the pursuers on horseback came to the river to cross it, the water became so swollen that it was quite impassable. Seeing this marvel, they went back home in astonishment, leaving the novice established in the order. So the brethren and the novice, seeing that their pursuers had gone home baffled, decided to return to St Dominic. And when they reached the river again to cross it, the water immediately returned to its place, presenting no hindrance to their passage. [Cecilia 11]

Although Dominic was psychologically well balanced, he did not abandon the ascetic means which could bring him ever greater freedom. Some of his ascetic practices shock us today, but they were entirely rooted in the religious mentality and cultural tradition of his time. Though his asceticism seemingly only affected the body, what he was aiming at by means of it was imperishable spiritual values; he wanted in this way to free himself from the world which perishes. Of himself he demanded much, but he was lenient towards his fellow human beings. He did not overburden them, and he had a sense of what each individual was able to bear. His shining countenance and his human radiance were due in part to his well-balanced asceticism.

(36)   When he was still a child, not yet taken out of his nurse's care, he was often found to have deserted his bed; as if he wanted to shun carnal self-indulgence, he preferred to lie on the ground rather than to relax in any kind of bodily repose in a bed. From that time onwards it was his custom to decline the soft comfort of bedding and to sleep most often on the

ground. He appeared to have understood the proverb he had not yet read, 'A young man will not depart from his way even when he grows old' (Prov. 22:6). [Petrus Ferrandi 5]

(37)　Brother Rudolph said that Brother Dominic always wore an iron chain round his loins, next to the skin, and he wore it like this until his death. Asked how he knew this, he replied that after his death he found it fastened round him, and he took it and kept it, though later he gave it to the Master of the Order, Master Jordan. He also said that at night he lay down dressed exactly as he had been for the day's walking, except that he took his shoes off, and sometimes he lay on the ground, sometimes on a hurdle, over which the witness used to place a cloth for him to lie on; very often he would sleep sitting up. [Bologna Canonisation Process 31]

(38)　Guillelme, the wife of Hélie Marty, said on oath that she did the sewing for a hair-shirt that was being prepared for him to wear. [Languedoc Canonisation Process 15]

(39)　Neguesa of Toulouse said on oath that she sewed him a hair-shirt made from the hair of pards[1] and goats. [Ibid. 16]

(40)　Beceda, a nun of Holy Cross, said on oath that she knew that all the items listed were true, and that she knew him to be a virgin. And she collected the tails of cows to make a hair-shirt for his use and one for Bishop Fulk of Toulouse. Although he made himself very much at home with her, she never heard any idle word from his mouth. Though she had often made up a bed for him, he never slept in it; on the contrary, she would find it still made in the morning, just as she had left it ready for him. And he did the same thing even when he was ill. She often found him sleeping on the ground with nothing to cover him. She used to put some covering over him, but when she returned she would find him praying, standing up or lying prostrate. She took great care of him. She also said that, though he had eaten more than two hundred times in the house in which she lived, at most he used to eat two eggs, even though several dishes were prepared for him. [Ibid. 17]

(41)   In the city of Segovia there was a woman, very devoted to God, with whom the saint of God, Dominic, used sometimes to stay. He left there a tunic made out of sacking which he had been using for a time in place of a hair-shirt, because he had found a very coarse hair-shirt which was prickly enough to satisfy him. The woman took this tunic devoutly and put it in a chest with her treasures and kept it more carefully than if it were royal purple. One day it chanced that the woman went out to do some business and left her house untended and shut up; because she was in a hurry or for some other reason she left a fire burning there, and the fire spread bit by bit and burned up everything that was on the floor of the house, except for the wooden chest in which the tunic was kept. Although it was right in the middle of the fire, it did not burn, in fact it was not even marked by the smoke. When the woman returned, she was amazed at such a miracle, and immediately gave thanks to God and to St Dominic, her guest, who had preserved from the fire not only his own tunic, but also all the little property she had, almost all of which was kept in this chest. Out of devotion she kept the sleeves of the tunic herself, but the rest of it she gave to the friars to keep, and to this day it is preserved as a relic in the friars' priory. [*Lives of the Brethren* II 9]

(42)   Brother Ventura said that, when [Dominic] was travelling, he used to lie down on straw to sleep, clothed and shod just as he was for walking during the day, except that he thinks he took his overshoes off. [Bologna Canonisation Process 3]

(43)   He also said that, when [Dominic] was on the road, he kept the fast the whole time from the feast of the Exaltation of the Cross until Easter, and in the summer too he observed all the fasts appointed by the church and every Friday. And

whatever food he was given when he was travelling he ate patiently, except that he did not eat meat or any dish with meat in it, nor did he knowingly eat anything cooked with dripping. And if he was badly served in food or drink while he was travelling he did not complain; on the contrary, it seemed to make him happy. He knows this because he saw it all when journeying with him. And when he was on a journey, whenever he arrived at a place where the brethren had a priory, he did not go and rest, as some people do, but called the brethren together and gave them a sermon and put the Word of God to them with much consolation. [Ibid. 4]

(44)   Brother William of Monferrato said that the whole time that he was with him he saw him following the rule of the Friars Preachers and their regular life most strictly. He made good use of dispensations with his brethren, but he never dispensed himself. He saw that he observed all the fasts laid down in the rule, whether he was in good health or bad. Going with him to Rome he saw him suffering from a serious illness, namely dysentery, and even that did not make him break his fast. Nor did he eat meat or have any extra dish prepared for him, except occasionally some fruit or turnip. [Ibid. 12]

(45)   Guillelme, the wife of Hélie Marty, said that he ate with her two hundred times and more, but she never saw him eat even a quarter of a piece of fish at one meal or more than two egg-yolks, or drink more than one cup of wine so diluted that it was three-quarters water, nor did she ever see him eat more than one crust of bread. She also saw that when he was in terrible pain, as he often was, he was put to bed by the other people present, but he at once prostrated himself on the ground, because he was not accustomed to lying in bed.

[Languedoc Canonisation Process 15]

(46)   Canon William Peire, abbot of St Paul's, said that [Dominic] was very sparing in the food he allowed himself,

eating no cooked dish but only bread and wine, except when he accepted a little of some extra dish for the sake of the brethren or the other people there. But he always wanted the other others to have plenty, as far as the resources of the house permitted. He also said that he declined the bishopric of Conserans and refused to take charge of it, even though he was elected to be its pastor and prelate. He also said that he was generous and hospitable and gladly shared whatever he had with the poor. He loved and respected religious and their friends. He also said that he never saw or heard of him having any bed except the church, where he could conveniently find a church; where there was no church available, he always lay on the ground or on a bench or else he would remove the mattress and bedding which had been supplied and lie down on the ropes of a bed. He also said that he always saw him using the same tunic, and it was full of patches. He always wanted to wear a cheaper cappa than the other brethren. He also said that he was a faithful supporter of the campaign for the faith and for peace and gave it all the help he could.

[Ibid. 18]

(47)   Brother Stephen said that Brother Dominic was sparing in food and drink. Asked how he knew this, he replied that in the refectory he often saw that, when the brethren were having two dishes, he contented himself with one. And, while the other brethren were eating, Brother Dominic nearly always slept at table because of his long vigils, which left him so tired, and he ate little and drank little, and this was why he was overtaken by sleep like this at table almost in spite of himself.

[Bologna Canonisation Process 38]

(48)   Brother Buonviso said that, when he wanted to discover the place where [Dominic] went to bed, he could not find that he had any place of his own to lie down in, as the other brethren had; instead, he was sometimes found sleeping on a bench, sometimes on the ground, sometimes on the ropes of

a chair or a stretcher. He also said that he lay down at night wearing the same clothes in which he had been walking about during the day. [Ibid. 20]

(49)   Brother John of Spain said that [Dominic] was sparing in food and drink, particularly when it came to special treats. Although he dispensed others, he always refused to dispense himself; on the contrary, he kept the whole rule strictly himself. Asked how he knows this, he replied that he saw it. He also said that when he was walking through towns and villages he scarcely raised his eyes from the ground, and he knows this because he walked with him through towns and villages and saw it. He also said that he had no place of his own to lie down in, as the other brethren did. Asked how he knew this, he replied that, if he had had a place of his own, the witness would certainly have been aware of it, particularly as he had tried hard to find out. He also said that on three occasions he was elected bishop and each time he refused, choosing to live with his brethren in poverty rather than to accept any bishopric.

[Ibid. 28]

(50)   Brother Paul of Venice said that once he went on a long journey with him, and one night St Dominic and the witness, with his companion, lodged at the parish church in Porto Legnago. The father, Dominic, had a place prepared for his companions to lie down, but he went into the church and spent the night there in prayer, and in spite of that he attended matins with the clergy of that church and with his companions. He also said that on the journey St Dominic fasted himself but made the companions who were with him eat because of the labour of travelling. [Ibid. 42]

(51)   When [Dominic] turned aside to some secular hostel after the labours of travelling, he first quenched his thirst at a spring or at any water that was nearby, because he was afraid it would make a bad impression if the thirst kindled by the

journey made him drink too much, and he was always extremely careful to avoid giving a bad impression.

[*Lives of the Brethren* II 24]

(52)   He held his love so firmly fixed on the Lord that he withdrew his affection from all worldly things, not only great things but even small, petty things like clothes and books and shoes, his belt, his knife and other such things which he wore or carried with him, and which were always cheap. He often rebuked fussiness or undue concern for appearances in such matters. [Ibid. II 25]

(53)   Brother Stephen of Metz said that the man of God, Dominic, ate and drank nothing but bread and water throughout the whole of that Lent [when he was the bishop's vicar in Carcassonne], nor did he sleep in a bed. But when Easter came he claimed to be stronger than ever and he looked more attractive and seemed to be in better condition than before. [Constantine 56]

(54)   While the crusaders were in the land, Brother Dominic remained there until the death of the Count de Montfort, constantly preaching the word of God. And how many insults he endured there from wicked men! How much plotting of theirs he made light of! On one occasion, finally, when they were threatening him with death, he replied calmly, 'I am not worthy of the glory of martyrdom, I have not yet merited such a death.' Later on, when he was passing by a place where he suspected that perhaps they were lying in wait for him, he went on his way singing cheerfully. When the heretics heard about this, they were astonished at his imperturbable firmness and asked him, 'Do you have no fear of death? What would you have done if we had caught you?' He said, 'I should have asked you not to strike me down quickly and kill me all at once, but to prolong my martyrdom by mutilating my limbs one by one, and then to display the mangled bits of my body before my

eyes, and then to gouge out my eyes and either leave what remained of my body wallowing in its own blood or finish me off completely; a slow martyrdom like that would win me a finer crown.' The enemies of truth were astounded to hear him talk like this. They stopped plotting against him and lying in wait for the just man's life (Ps. 93:21), because they realised that if they killed him they would be doing him a favour rather than harming him. For his part Brother Dominic, with all his energy and with passionate zeal, set himself to win all the souls he could for Christ. His heart was full of an extraordinary, almost incredible, yearning for the salvation of everyone.

[Jordan, *Libellus* 34]

(55) At that time the blessed Dominic remained there until the death of the Count de Montfort, constantly proclaiming the word of God, nor was he denied the apostolic glory of being found worthy to suffer insult for the name of Jesus (Acts 5:41). The heretics mocked the holy man and made fun of him in all kinds of ways, spitting at him and throwing mud and other such filth at him. One of them was later moved by repentance to come and say in confession that he had struck St Dominic by throwing mud at him and that he had fastened straw to his back to make him ridiculous. But, as if this were not enough, they lay in wait for the just man's life (Ps. 93:21) and plotted his death, and with sacrilegious tongues they aimed villainous threats at him. But the soldier of Christ made light of them, magnanimous in his faith, and he said to the people who were threatening him, 'I am not worthy of martyrdom, I have not yet merited such a death.' And when, on one occasion, he was passing a place in which he suspected they were lying in wait for him, he went on his way, not merely fearlessly, but singing cheerfully, following the example of Christ, of whom it says, 'He was offered because he willed it' (Is. 53:7).

[Petrus Ferrandi 20]

(56) On one occasion a public debate was organised against

the heretics. The place they were going to was many miles away, and on the way there they began to be uncertain of their route, so they asked for directions from someone they thought was a catholic, but in fact he was a heretic. 'Certainly,' he said, 'not only will I show you the way, I shall be delighted to escort you there in person.' While he was taking them through a wood somewhere, he led them astray so viciously, through thorns and thistles, that their feet and legs became quite covered in blood. The man of God endured all this with the utmost patience; breaking out into a hymn of praise to God, he encouraged the others to praise God too and to be patient. 'My friends,' he said, 'hope in the Lord. Victory will be ours, because even now our sins are being washed away in blood.' The heretic saw their extraordinary and cheerful patience and was pricked with compunction at the good words spoken by the man of God, so he admitted the poisonous way he had deceived them and renounced his heresy. When they reached the place of the debate, everything came to a satisfactory conclusion.

[*Lives of the Brethren* II 2]

(57)   Asked once why he did not choose to live in Toulouse and the diocese of Toulouse rather than in Carcassonne and its diocese, he said, 'Because in the diocese of Toulouse I find many people treat me with respect, whereas in Carcassonne they all criticise me.' [Constantine 62]

(58)   It often happened that they were caught in the rain while travelling, and his and his companions' clothes would get very wet. After dinner, while his companions remained by the fire to hold their clothes out to dry and to refresh their bodies a little, the man of God, Dominic, ablaze with the fire of the Holy Spirit, would immediately go into the church to pray, as was his custom, or rather to spend the whole night in prayer, just as he was, however wet his clothes might be. But in the morning, though the clothes of the others who had stayed by

the fire were still wet, his would be found as thoroughly dry as if they had been in a warm oven all night. [Constantine 42]

As an intelligent man Dominic was humble, because he was aware of his own human limitations and recognised the limitations of others. Consequently he respected the differences there are between people and between their ideas and was ready to enter into dialogue with others and to make concessions to them; in this way, in his humility, he could endure colliding with reality, unyielding as it often is. His humility expressed itself in a readiness to serve others, but he also appreciated the services which were rendered to him and was grateful for them. It was precisely his humble and grateful attitude which made him congenial to others, so that he had numerous friends. They could give him their confidence because he was dependable, so that an enduring relationship could develop.

(59)   Brother Ventura said that he heard his confession during the illness which resulted in his going to the Lord. He made a general confession of all that he had done, in the presence and hearing of many priests. It is his belief that he never committed a mortal sin and that he was always a virgin, and the reason for this belief is this general confession which he heard. Afterwards he said to the witness privately, 'Brother, I have sinned, because I have spoken publicly about my virginity in the presence of the brethren, which I ought not to have done.'

[Bologna Canonisation Process 5]

(60)   He also said that, while Dominic was seriously ill, they had him taken to Santa Maria del Monte, which was a healthier place. And, when he thought he was dying, he sent for the prior and the brethren. About twenty friars went there with the prior. When they were gathered round him, he began to preach to them from his bed and he gave them an excellent and moving sermon. The witness never heard a more inspiring sermon from his lips. And he thinks that it was then that they anointed him. At that time he also heard that the monk who

was currently in charge of the church there had said that, if he died there, he would not allow him to be taken away, but would have him buried in the church there. When the prior reported this to Brother Dominic, Brother Dominic replied, 'God forbid that I should be buried anywhere except under the feet of my brethren. Carry me outside, so that I may die in that vineyard, so that you can bury me in our church.'

[Bologna Canonisation Process 8]

(61)   Brother Rudolph said that during Brother Dominic's last sickness, from which he died, the brethren were gathered round him and were weeping. The witness was holding his head with a towel and was wiping the sweat from his face. Brother Dominic said, 'Do not weep, because I shall be more useful to you in the place where I am going than I have been here.' Asked who was present at the time, he replied that many of the brethren were there, but he does not remember their names. He also said that one of the brethren asked him, 'Father, where do you want your body to be buried?', and he said, 'Under the feet of my brethren.' He also said that he firmly believes that when the brethren who were saying the office of the commendation of his soul reached the words, 'Come to help him, saints of God, run to meet him, angels of the Lord, taking his soul and presenting it in the sight of the Most High', that was when he breathed his last. And he said that he never saw him lying on a feather bed or even on a pallet except at the time of his death, because then he was lying on a pallet. He also said that when Brother Dominic was at the point of death he said to the brethren, 'Get ready', and they went and got themselves ready, and while the commendation of his soul was being said he breathed his last, holding his hands up towards heaven.

[Ibid. 33]

(62)   In this way the servant of God, Dominic, advanced in virtue and in his reputation, and the heretics became jealous. In proportion to his goodness they looked more and more

askance at him. Their bleary eyes could not stand the brilliance of his light. But they made mock of him and followed him round, teasing him in various ways, bringing forth evil from the evil treasure in their hearts (Matt. 12:35). But, while unbelievers mocked, the faithful were filled with devout joy because of him. All the catholics felt such respect for him that even the hearts of the nobility were touched by the charm of his holiness and the attractiveness of his character. And the archibishops and bishops and other prelates in the area considered him worthy of the highest honour. [Jordan, *Libellus* 36]

(63)   Count de Montfort was particularly devoted to him; with his men's consent he gave an important estate called Casseneuil to him and his followers and to those who were helping him in the mission of salvation which had been started there.

[Ibid. 37]

(64)   Bishop Fulk of Toulouse, of happy memory, was very fond of Brother Dominic, who was 'beloved of God and men' (Ecclus. 45:1), because he saw the brethren's religious way of life and the grace they had and their fervour in preaching, and he rejoiced at the appearance of this new light. So, with the consent of his whole Chapter, he granted them a sixth of all the tithes of his diocese to enable them to obtain what they needed in the way of books and food. [Ibid. 39]

(65)   Brother Ventura said that, as he believed, it was by the kindness and providence of God that the Lord Bishop of Ostia, Ugolino, who is now pope, and the Lord Patriarch of Aquileia and many venerable bishops and abbots were present at his burial. The Lord Bishop of Ostia (now pope) celebrated the Mass himself and the commendation of his soul, and he performed the funeral. He said that, on the recent feast of St Sixtus, it was exactly twelve years since he passed to the Lord.

[Bologna Canonisation Process 8]

(66)   Brother William of Monferrato said that sixteen years ago or so he went to the city of Rome to spend Lent there, and the present pope, who was then Bishop of Ostia, received him into his home. Brother Dominic, the founder and first Master of the Order of Preachers, was at the Roman curia at that time and he often visited the house of the Lord Bishop of Ostia. This was how the witness came to know him then, and Brother Dominic's way of life pleased him and he began to love him. He often discussed with him matters relating to their own salvation and that of other people. [Ibid. 12]

(67)   The Lord William, Bishop of Sabina, was a great friend of the Order and of St Dominic from the very beginning; he had become intimate with him in the papal curia.

[Anonymous Chronicle of the Order, MOPH I p. 334]

(68)   The Lord William, at that time Bishop of Modena, but now Cardinal Bishop of Sabina, studied the behaviour of St Dominic and asked to be received by him as a brother in the order. The saint granted him this and entrusted the order's affairs to him as to a father. And the bishop has been enthusiastic in carrying out this function ever since.

[Bartholomew of Trent 17]

ᴖ 6 ᴖ

SPEAKING WITH GOD

As a canon, Dominic was formed by the church's great tradition of prayer which, in addition to the official liturgical prayer, cultivated private spiritual reading combined with meditation (*lectio divina*). Life in the house of canons at Osma had a pre-eminently contemplative orientation. Supported by recollection and silence, it aimed to foster the attentive reception of the word of God and its deep personal assimilation. As a member of the community of canons Dominic already lived entirely by that gospel, which penetrated his contemplation. Later, when he was constantly on the road, he continued in habitual union with God. Prayer and work, thought and action formed a unity in him. Everything was grounded in the love of God. It was from prayer and meditation that Dominic derived the vital force of his ministry to his fellow human beings, to the church and to the world, thus permitting a more authentic, a more attractive image of this church to emerge in the eyes of his contemporaries.

Prayer was for him a part of the realisation of the current maxim of the apostolic life, 'By word and example' (*verbo et exemplo*), and of his personal motto, 'To speak with God or about God'. He arranged for the insertion of this motto into the constitutions of his order.[1] The saying is attributed already to the hermit, Stephen of Muret († 1124). Dominic however gave it a completely new colouring. While for St Stephen speaking about God was necessary only when it happened that his hermits had to be in contact with outsiders, for Dominic it represented the essential task and goal of his order. However, speaking of God is preceded by speaking with God, though they can never be separated from one another. Since his word sprang from the inner experience he had with God in prayer, it was always a testimony backed by his own life, a consonance which was necessary if his word was to reach his hearers. As the evidence of the Canonisation Process shows, his prayer was permeated by the entire gamut of emotions, from cheerfulness to grief. But Dominic did not get bogged down at the emotional level, he was constantly stirred to action through prayer. Prayer gave him the courageous confidence and inner certainty to make decisions without hesitation, so that his contemporaries attributed his conduct to inspired revelation. Because his humanly clear-sighted and accurate assessment of reality was increasingly sharpened in prayer and contemplation, it appeared, in the judgement of those around him, to be supported by prophetic vision. He strode towards the future, not with any Stoic attitude of resigning himself to what had to be, but with a firm determination, which communicated itself to other people.

(69) Brother Ventura said that when [Dominic] was travelling he celebrated Mass almost every day, if he found a church. And while he was singing the Mass he used to shed many tears, as the witness saw. And, when he arrived at a hostel, if there was a church there, he always went to pray in it. And almost always, when he was not in a priory, he would get up and rouse the brethren when he heard the first bell for matins being rung in the monasteries; and he would celebrate the whole Divine Office, the day hours and the night office, with great devotion, omitting nothing. And after compline he kept silence and made his companions do likewise, going on their way as if they were in a priory. [Bologna Canonisation Process 3]

(70) Brother William of Monferrato said that, whenever it was time for [Dominic] to go to bed, he first applied himself energetically to prayer, sometimes with groans and tears, so that often he woke the witness and the others from sleep with his groaning and weeping. And he firmly believes that he spent more time in prayer than in sleeping. And the whole time the witness was with him he always lay down fully clothed, with his cappa and his belt on and wearing his shoes. And he always lay down without a mattress, on the ground or on a plank or on some kind of straw. He always observed silence at the

customary times prescribed in religious life. He refrained from idle words and spoke always about God or with God.

[Ibid. 13]

(71) Brother Buonviso said that, when the brethren left the church after compline to go to sleep, it was Brother Dominic's custom to hide in the church to pray. The witness wanted to find out what Brother Dominic was doing in church, so he often hid in the church and listened to him praying to the Lord with immense shouting and weeping and great groans. Asked how he knew that it was Brother Dominic, he replied that he saw him, since there was a light in the church, and he also recognised him by his voice, so that he is quite certain it was Brother Dominic. He also said that he firmly believes that he often used to spend the whole night in church, and this was well known among the brethren. [Ibid. 20]

(72) Brother John of Spain said that Brother Dominic was assiduous in prayer by day and by night. He also said that he prayed more than the other brethren with whom he lived, and also kept vigil more and took the discipline on his body more severely and more often than the rest. The witness knows this because he very often saw him doing all this. [Ibid. 25]

(73) Brother Rudolph said that it was Brother Dominic's habit very frequently to spend the whole night in church. He prayed a lot, and in his prayer he wept with tears and much groaning. Asked how he knows this, he replied that he very often used to follow him in church, and he saw it. He often stayed with him at night and he frequently saw him praying like this and heard him weeping. And he often saw him, when he was praying, standing on the tips of his toes, and he would hold his hands raised, as in prayer. Asked how he saw him if it was night, he replied that there was always a light in church. And the witness used to set himself to pray beside him, because he was very intimate with him. And he said confidently that he

was very devout and more persistent in prayer than anyone else he had ever seen. [Ibid. 31]

(74) He also said that, whether at home or on a journey, [Dominic] always wanted to speak about God or the salvation of souls. Nor did he ever hear from his mouth any idle or harmful word or anything disparaging. [Ibid. 32]

(75) Brother Stephen said that it was [Dominic's] custom always to speak about God or with God, in the house or outside or when he was travelling. And he encouraged the brethren to do the same and put it in his constitutions too. He was more persistent and devout in prayer than anyone else the witness has ever seen. And, as the witness says he observed, he habitually made everyone else go into the dormitory after compline and the customary prayer that the brethren make, but he himself stayed behind to pray in the church. And at night, while he prayed, he was so moved and broke out into such groaning and weeping that the brethren who were nearby were woken from their sleep, and some of them moved to tears. Very often he spent the whole night in prayer, up to the time for matins, and all the same he was there for matins, going round both sides of choir, urging and encouraging them to sing loudly and with devotion. His habit of spending the night in prayer was such that the witness never remembers seeing him sleep in a bed at night, although he had spent so much time with him in the same priory and had very often investigated carefully to see if he could ever discover him in bed – though there was actually a place set aside for him to lie down, where there was just a cover spread over a stretcher, with no straw or mattress. [Ibid. 37]

(76) Brother Paul of Venice said that, when he was with him on a journey, he saw him either praying or preaching, or he would devote himself to prayer or to thinking about God. Asked how he knows this, he replied that Master Dominic

used to say to him and to the others who were with him, 'You go ahead, and let us think about our Saviour.' And he would hear him groaning and sighing. He also said that wherever the Master was he always spoke about God or with God, and he encouraged the brethren to do the same and had it written into the rule of the Friars Preachers. [Ibid. 41]

(77)   In praying [Dominic] wept a lot, and he knows this because he often saw him doing it. And sometimes he called him from prayer and saw his face wet with tears. He also said that he was devout and persistent in prayer even when he was travelling. And every day he wanted to sing Mass, if he could find a suitable church. [Ibid. 42]

(78)   Brother Frugerio said that [Dominic] was persistent and devoted in prayer, whether he was on a journey or in a priory, so that he was never able to find him sleeping in a bed, although one was sometimes prepared for him, whether he was on the road or in a priory. Sometimes, worn out by staying awake too much at night, he would prop himself up or lie down on the ground or on a piece of wood and go to sleep. [Ibid. 46]

(79)   Canon William Peire said that he had never seen a man who frequented prayer so assiduously, nor anyone who had such an abundant flow of tears. He also said that, when he was at prayer, he used to shout to such an extent that he could be heard everywhere. And what he used to shout was this: 'Lord, have mercy on your people. What are sinners going to do?' In this way he spent his nights without sleep, weeping and sobbing for the sins of others. [Languedoc Canonisation Process 18]

(80)   Brother John of Bologna, a good man, of sound judgement, said that he had kept watch for seven nights to see how the blessed father comported himself at night. So he said that he persevered in prayer, now standing, now kneeling, now prostrate, until he was overcome by sleep. As soon as he woke

up again, he began visiting the altars. He went on like this until about midnight. Then he very quietly visited the sleeping brethren, covering any of them who were uncovered. Having done this, he returned to the church and began praying again at once. The same brother said that he frequently assisted him at Mass and saw that tears were often flowing from his eyes when he turned to take the wine and water after receiving the Lord's Body. [*Lives of the Brethren* II 18]

(81)   The holy father was also an 'Israel', seeing God by contemplation. A single example makes this clear, which has so far eluded the hands of the reapers (Ruth 2:2). The blessed father often used to like visiting places of prayer and the bodies of the saints, and he did not just pass by like a cloud without rain; he often stayed there in prayer, making no distinction between night and day. In particular, whenever he had the chance, he used to break his journey at a town called Castres, in the diocese of Albi, which is next to the diocese of Toulouse, out of reverence and respect for the blessed deacon, Vincent, whose body, as is well known and quite certain, has been resting there since the time of Charlemagne. In the manner of the French church Count de Montfort, when he was the lord of this territory, established secular prebends in the church there. The prior was Brother Matthew, who was later the first and last abbot in the Order of Preachers. At the time when he was prior, St Dominic, as was his custom, remained in church after Mass, praying in front of the altar. When midday came and lunch was ready and the table laid, the prior sent one of the clerics to call the saint. Going into the church he saw St Dominic in the air, some eight or nine inches above the ground, not touching it at all. Unnerved and amazed at the sight, he informed the prior, who waited for some time and then finally went himself and saw the saint about a foot and a half above the ground. He waited until he returned from his heavenly home to his bodily dwelling place and was lying prostrate before the altar. Because of what he had seen the prior shortly

afterwards became a follower of St Dominic, who promised the bread of life and the water of heaven to him and to all those whom he received – the blessed father always made this promise when he received people into the order and gave them the habit. [Stephen of Salagnac I 9]

ST DOMINIC'S BODILY WAY OF PRAYING

This little treatise, commonly known as *The Nine Ways of Prayer of St Dominic*, was almost certainly compiled in its present form by the Italian Dominican who edited and adapted Dietrich of Apolda's life of St Dominic, some time between 1297 and 1308, on the basis of earlier material. We can only guess how much he himself added. It is noticeable, however, that the bulk of the text presents a remarkably sober account of Dominic's prayer, in stark contrast to the flamboyant account, derived from Cecilia, of the miraculous resuscitation of Cardinal Stephen's nephew, and the rather bizarre tales concerning the sacristan of Bologna. It is also evident that the compiler, in dividing the text into nine distinct Ways, has to some extent distorted the structure of the underlying source; the distinction between the eighth and ninth Ways is particularly unfortunate, as they clearly describe the same Way and most of what is said in the ninth Way is intended to apply equally to the eighth. The two Ways taken together exemplify the Dominican insistence on constant reading and meditation, at home and on the road (cf. 170).

It is certain that the compiler intended the work to be illustrated, and he probably took steps to see that a fair copy, with pictures, was deposited in Bologna, which was the natural and official centre for the cult of Dominic, since that was where his tomb was. But this fair copy no longer exists.

By 1308 the text was known in the south of France, where a beautifully illustrated manuscript of the *Nine Ways* was produced for the Carthusian monastery of Porta Caeli in Valencia; the manuscript is now in the Vatican Library (Rossianus 3). These pictures have often been reproduced.

Early in the fourteenth century the work was translated into Castilian, and there is an illustrated manuscript of this translation in the monastery of Santo Domingo el Real in Madrid. In the fifteenth century an Italian adaptation was made in Bologna, expanding the text to include fourteen ways of prayer; the manuscript of this adaptation has unfortunately been lost, but photographs of its illustrations have been published. Fra Angelico's portrayal of St Dominic in the cells of San Marco, Florence, is profoundly influenced by the *Nine Ways*.[2]

Dominic prayed as a whole man, body and soul together, with no division between them. The *Nine Ways* shows this strikingly. With Dominic nothing happens in the spirit without the participation of the body, and nothing happens in the body without the spirit. Thus posture and meaning are at one in him, even in prayer, and this is reflected in his whole body. Different bodily postures correspond to different kinds of prayer (e.g. meditation, adoration, petition, contemplation etc.). Specific intentions in prayer find expression in an appropriate bodily posture. Even the intentions of a contemplative are often apostolic.

What is most impressive in the description of the Ways of prayer is the attempt to express closeness to the gospel and to the psalms through a definite posture in prayer. The text also distinguishes clearly between a fundamental stance of living the gospel, which Dominic taught chiefly by his example, and what the order received from him as forms of prayer. It is easy to see why his example had such a strong impact.

The 'William' mentioned in the prologue is William Peraldus OP author of the *Summa on Vices and Virtues* which was one of the best-known religious books of the time, which Humbert of Romans advised every Dominican house to have in its library. It was completed by about 1250 and well over 100 manuscripts of it survive from the thirteenth century alone. More than one passage from its treatise on prayer is quoted in the *Nine Ways*.

In the first Way of Prayer, it should be noticed that it is the altar itself which is the symbol of Christ. As yet it was not the common practice to have the Blessed Sacrament reserved in a tabernacle on the altar.

It is difficult for us today to enter into the spirit of the third Way.

The use of the discipline to beat oneself is a practice which arose in the tenth century and subsequently came to be widely adopted. It is interesting that the first constitutions of the Order of Preachers, which were drawn up under Dominic, do not prescribe the use of the discipline, which is mentioned merely as a penance for quite specific faults.

Dominic sent even novices out to preach, which shows his great confidence in the working of the Holy Spirit, which he besought for them in prayer, as the fourth Way informs us.

The eighth Way alludes to what was by this time the classic sequence of elements in contemplative practice: reading, meditation, prayer and contemplation. Dominic's spiritual freedom and maturity is hinted at in the remark that he passed straight from reading to prayer or from meditation to contemplation, rather than proceeding through all four elements in order. Reading (*lectio*) is an important feature of this spiritual way, as we can see also in the paintings of Fra Angelico.

The anecdotes in the seventh and ninth Ways are likely to strike a modern reader as somewhat preposterous. But the sacristan whom they concern is a convincing human character – and we may be sure that he learned his lesson that misplaced flippancy, if not nipped in the bud, may in the long run lead to a disastrous coarsening of one's sensibility. And, even if we doubt whether it was really the devil's confession that St Dominic heard, it is not difficult to believe that on some occasion there was a penitent so appalling that only a priest with Dominic's stamina could bear to hear him out. And we know from other sources that Dominic was completely unafraid and even brutal in facing up to the devil and all his works, and that, when necessary, he was a stern disciplinarian, even though he managed to combine this with such evident compassion that people went away strengthened and comforted, not downhearted, from his severe ministrations. What but prayer could lie behind such unusual gifts?

(82) The holy doctors Augustine, Leo, Ambrose, Gregory, Hilary, Isidore, John Chrysostom and John Damascene and Bernard and other devout teachers, both Greeks and Latins, have spoken extensively about prayer, recommending it and

describing it, telling us how necessary and useful it is, how to do it and how to prepare for it, as well as indicating the obstacles that may arise. In addition to these, the renowned and glorious teacher, Brother Thomas Aquinas, and William and Albert, of the Order of Preachers, have expounded the subject nobly and systematically, devoutly and attractively, in their treatment of the Virtues in their various books.

However, what we must say something about here is the way of praying in which the soul uses the members of the body in order to rise more devotedly to God, so that the soul, as it causes the body to move, is in turn moved by the body, until sometimes it comes to be in ecstasy like Paul (2 Cor. 12:2–4), sometimes in agony like our Saviour (Luke 22:43), and sometimes in rapture like the prophet David (Ps. 30:23). The blessed Dominic used often to pray like this.

We find, in fact, that the holy men of the Old and New Testaments sometimes prayed like this. This manner of praying stirs up devotion, the soul stirring the body and the body stirring the soul. Praying this way used to make St Dominic dissolve utterly into weeping, and it so kindled the fervour of his good will that his mind could not prevent his bodily members from showing unmistakable signs of his devotion. So, by the sheer force of his mind at prayer, he sometimes rose up in petitions and entreaties and thanksgiving (1 Tim. 2:1).

Apart from the common ways of prayer in the celebration of the Mass and in the prayer of psalmody in the canonical hours, which he practised very devoutly both in choir and when he was travelling, and during which he often seemed suddenly to be caught up above himself to speak with God and the angels, his ways of praying were as follows.

The first way of prayer

First of all, bowing humbly before the altar as if Christ, whom the altar signifies, were really and personally present and not just symbolically. As it says, 'The prayer of the person who

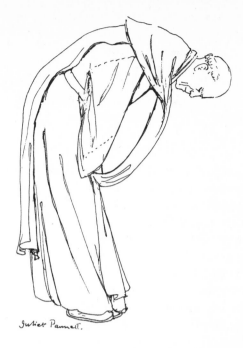

Juliet Pannett.

humbles himself will pierce the clouds' (Ecclus. 35:21). He used sometimes to say to the brethren the text from Judith, 'The prayer of the humble and meek has always been pleasing to you' (Jud. 9:16). It was by humility that the Canaanite woman obtained what she wanted (Matt. 15:22–28), and so did the prodigal son (Luke 15:18–24). Also, 'I am not worthy to have you come under my roof' (Matt. 8:8). 'Lord, humble my spirit deeply because, Lord, I am utterly humbled before you' (Ecclus. 7:19, Ps. 118:107). So the holy father, standing with his body erect, would bow his head and his heart humbly before Christ his Head, considering his own servile condition and the outstanding nobility of Christ, and giving himself up entirely to venerating him.

He taught the brethren to do this whenever they passed before a crucifix showing the humiliation of Christ, so that Christ, who was humbled for our sake, might particularly see

93

us humbled before his greatness. Similarly he told the brethren to humble themselves like this before the whole Trinity whenever 'Glory be to the Father and to the Son and to the Holy Spirit' was recited solemnly.

This way of prayer, as illustrated in the picture, was the beginning of his devotion: bowing deeply.

The second way of prayer

St Dominic also often used to pray throwing himself down on the ground, flat on his face, and then his heart would be pricked with compunction and he would blush at himself and say, sometimes loudly enough for it actually to be heard, the words from the gospel, 'Lord, be merciful to me, a sinner' (Luke 18:13). And with great devotion and reverence he would recite the words of David, 'It is I who have sinned and done unjustly' (2 Sam. 24:17). He would weep and groan passionately and then say, 'I am not worthy to look upon the height of heaven, because of the greatness of my sin; I have provoked your anger and done evil in your sight' (Prayer of Manasseh 9–10). He would also say, emphatically and devoutly, the verse from Psalm 43:25, 'My soul is laid low in the dust, my belly is stuck to the earth.' And again, 'My soul is stuck to the floor, make me come alive according to your word' (Ps. 118:25).

Sometimes, wanting to teach the brethren with what reverence they ought to pray, he would say to them, 'The Magi, those devout kings, entered the house and found the child with Mary, his mother (Matt. 2:11). Now it is certain that we have

found him too, God and man, with Mary his handmaid, so come, let us fall down and worship before God, let us weep before the Lord who made us' (Ps. 94:6).

He exhorted the young men too, saying to them, 'If you cannot weep for your own sins, because you have none, still there are many sinners to be directed towards mercy and love, for whose sake the prophets and apostles groaned in distress, and for their sake too Jesus wept bitterly when he saw them (Luke 19:41), and similarly the holy David wept and said, "I saw the half-hearted and I pined away" ' (Ps. 118:158).

The third way of prayer

For this reason, rising up from the ground, he used to take the discipline with an iron chain saying, 'Your discipline has set

me straight towards my goal' (Ps. 17:36). This is why the whole
order determined that all the brethren, out of respect for the
memory of St Dominic's example, should take the discipline
on their bare backs with sticks of wood every ferial day after
compline, saying the *Miserere* or the *De profundis*. They were
to do this either for their own sins or for those of others
whose gifts support them. So no one, however innocent, should
withdraw himself from following this holy example.

The fourth way of prayer

After this, St Dominic, standing before the altar or in the
chapter room, would fix his gaze on the crucifix, looking
intently at Christ on the cross and kneeling down over and
over again, a hundred times perhaps; sometimes he would
even spend the whole time from after compline until midnight
getting up and kneeling down again, like the apostle James,
and like the leper in the gospel who knelt down and said,
'Lord, if you will, you can make me clean' (Mark 1:40), and
like Stephen who knelt down and cried out with a loud voice,
'Lord, do not hold this sin against them' (Acts 7:59). And
a great confidence would grow in our holy father Dominic,
confidence in God's mercy for himself and for all sinners, and
for the protection of the novices whom he used to send out all
over the place to preach to souls. And sometimes he could not
contain his voice, but the brethren would hear him saying, 'To
you, Lord, I will cry, do not turn away from me in silence, lest
in your silence I become like those who go down into the pit'
(Ps. 27:1), and other such words from sacred scripture.

At other times, however, he spoke in his heart and his voice
was not heard at all (1 Sam. 1:13), and he would remain quietly
on his knees, his mind caught up in wonder, and this sometimes
lasted a long time. Sometimes it seemed from the very way he
looked that he had penetrated heaven in his mind, and then
he would suddenly appear radiant with joy, wiping away the
abundant tears running down his face. At such times he would

come to be in an intensity of desire, like a thirsty man coming to a spring of water (Ecclus. 26:15), or a traveller at last approaching his own country. Then he would grow more forceful and insistent, and his movements would display great composure and agility as he stood up and knelt down.

He was so accustomed to genuflecting that, when he was on a journey, whether in a hostel after the toils of the road or on the road itself, while the others were sleeping or resting, he would return to his genuflexions as to his own special art and his own personal service. This way of prayer he taught more by the example of his practice than by what he said.

The fifth way of prayer

Sometimes, when he was in a priory, our holy father Dominic would stand upright before the altar, not leaning on anything

Juliet Pannett.

or supported by anything, but with his whole body standing erect on his feet. Sometimes he would hold his hands out, open, before his breast, like an open book, and then he would stand with great reverence and devotion, as if he were reading in the presence of God. At such times he seemed to be meditating, savouring the words of God in his mouth and, as it were, enjoying reciting them to himself. He had made his own the Lord's practice which we read about in Luke 4:16, 'Jesus went into the synagogue on the sabbath day, as it was his custom to do, and stood up to read.' And it says in Psalm 105:30, 'Phineas stood and prayed and the pestilence stopped.'

At other times he joined his hands and held them tightly

fastened together in front of his eyes, hunching himself up. At other times he raised his hands to his shoulders, in the manner of a priest saying Mass, as if he wanted to fix his ears more attentively on something that was being said to him by someone else. If you had seen his devotion as he stood there, erect in prayer, you would have thought you were looking at a prophet conversing with an angel or with God, now talking, now listening, now thinking quietly about what had been revealed to him.

When he was travelling, he would steal sudden moments of prayer, unobtrusively, and would stand with his whole mind instantanenously concentrated on heaven, and soon you would have heard him pronouncing, with the utmost enjoyment and relish, some lovely text from the very heart of sacred scripture, which he would seem to have drawn fresh from the Saviour's wells (Is. 12:3).

The brethren used to be greatly moved by this example, when they saw their father and master praying in this way, and the more devout among them found it the best possible instruction in how to pray continuously and reverently, 'as the eyes of a handmaid are on the hands of her mistress and as the eyes of servants are on the hands of their masters' (Ps. 122:2), as the illustration makes clear.

The sixth way of prayer

Sometimes, as I was told personally by someone who had seen it, our holy father Dominic was also seen praying with his hands and arms spread out like a cross, stretching himself to the limit and standing as upright as he possibly could. This was how he prayed when God restored the boy Napoleon to life at his prayer at San Sisto in Rome, both in the sacristy and in the church during the Mass in which he rose from the ground, as we were told by that devout and holy sister, Cecilia, who was present with a great crowd of others and saw it all. Like

Juliet Pannett.

Elijah when he raised the widow's son, he stretched himself out over the boy's body (1 Kings 17:21).

He also prayed in the same way when he rescued the English pilgrims near Toulouse, when they were nearly drowned in the river (cf. 97).

This was how the Lord prayed when he hung on the cross, his hands and arms stretched out, when, with great cries and weeping, his prayer was heard because of his reverence (Heb. 5:7).

The holy man of God, Dominic, did not use this kind of prayer regularly, but only when, by God's inspiration, he knew that some great wonder was going to occur by virtue of his prayer. He neither forbade the brethren to pray like this nor did he encourage it.

When he raised the boy from the dead, praying standing with his arms and hands stretched out like a cross, we do not know what he said. Perhaps he used the words of Elijah, 'Lord my God, I beseech you, let the soul of this boy return within him' (1 Kings 17:21), just as he followed his manner of praying. But the brethren and the sisters and the cardinals and the rest who were there were paying attention to his manner of praying, which was unfamiliar and remarkable to them, and so they did not take in the words he spoke. And afterwards they could not ask the holy and extraordinary man, Dominic, about it, because in this deed he had shown himself to be an object of awe and reverence to them all.

However he did sometimes recite seriously, deliberately and carefully, the texts from the Psalms which refer to this manner of praying, such as Psalm 87:10, 'I cried to you, Lord, all day long I have stretched out my hands to you' with the rest of that psalm, and Psalm 142:6–7, 'I have stretched out my hands to you, my soul is like soil without water before you, speedily hear me, Lord'.

This makes it possible for anyone who prays devoutly to understand the teaching of this father, praying this way when he desired to be extraordinarily moved towards God, or rather, when he felt himself being moved by God in a particularly expansive way, through some hidden inspiration, in view of some special grace for himself or for somebody else, on the basis of David's doctrine, Elijah's symbolism, Christ's love and Dominic's devotion, as the illustration makes clear.

The seventh way of prayer

He was also often found stretching his whole body up towards heaven in prayer, like a choice arrow shot straight up from a bow (Is. 49:2). He had his hands stretched right up above his head, joined together or slightly open as if to catch something from heaven. And it is believed that at such times he received an increase of grace and was caught up in rapture, and that his

prayer won from God, for the order he had founded, the gifts of the Holy Spirit and, for himself and for his brethren, such delight and enjoyment in putting the Beatitudes into practice that each one would consider himself blessed in the most profound poverty, in bitter grief, in severe persecution, in great hunger and thirst for righteousness, in all the cares and worries of mercy (Matt. 5:3–10), and that they would all consider it a pleasure to observe the commandments with devotion and to follow the evangelical counsels. At such times the holy father seemed suddenly to enter the Holy of Holies and the third heaven (2 Cor. 12:2). And so, after this kind of prayer, he bore himself like a prophet, as is related in his miracles, whether he was rebuking or dispensing or preaching. Just one example must be given here, briefly, for edification's sake.

Once at Bologna, after praying like this, the holy master

Dominic asked the advice of some of the senior brethren about some decision that had to be made. This was his normal practice because, as he said, something may be shown to one good man which is not shown to another, as can be seen in the prophets. The sacristan then came and called one of the people taking part in this council to go to the women's church, to hear a confession, I think. He added, stupidly, though not, as he thought, loudly enough to be heard by the holy master Dominic, 'A beautiful lady is asking for you; come at once.' Then the Spirit came upon St Dominic and he began to be disturbed in himself, and the councillors looked at him with fear. Then he told the sacristan to come to him and he asked him, 'What did you say?' He replied, 'I was asking for a priest to come to the church.' And the father said, 'Reproach yourself and confess the sin which came to your lips. The God who made all things made me aware of what you thought were your secret words.' And he disciplined him there severely and long, so that those who were present were moved to compassion because of his bruises. Then he said, 'Go, my son; now you have learned how to gaze at a woman in the future. Make sure you do not judge of her appearance. And you too should pray that God will give you chaste eyes.' In this way he knew what was hidden, rebuked the brother's folly and punished him and taught him, as he had foreseen it all in prayer. And the brethren were amazed that this was what he said had to be done. And the holy master said, 'All our justice, by comparison with that of God, is nothing better than filth' (Is. 64:6).

So the holy father did not remain long in this kind of prayer, but returned to himself as if he were coming from far away, and at such times he seemed to be a stranger in the world, as could easily be seen from his appearance and his behaviour. While he was praying he was sometimes clearly heard by the brethren saying, as the prophet did, 'Hear the voice of my supplication while I pray to you and while I lift up my hands to your holy temple' (Ps. 27:2).

And the holy master taught the brethren to pray like this,

both by his words and by his example. He quoted from Psalm 133:2, 'At night lift up your hands to the holy place,' and Psalm 140:2, 'The raising of my hands like an evening sacrifice'. The illustration makes it clearer what this means.

The eighth way of prayer

The holy father Dominic also had another beautiful way of praying, full of devotion and grace. After the canonical hours and the grace which is said in common after meals the father would go off quickly to some place where he could be alone, in a cell or somewhere. Sober and alert and anointed with a spirit of devotion which he had drawn from the words of God which had been sung in choir or during the meal, he would settle himself down to read or pray, recollecting himself in himself and fixing himself in the presence of God. Sitting there quietly, he would open some book before him, arming himself first with the sign of the cross, and then he would read. And he would be moved in his mind as delightfully as if he heard the Lord speaking to him. As the Psalm says, 'I will hear what the Lord God is saying in me, because he will speak peace to his people and upon his saints, and to those who turn to him with all their heart' (Ps. 84:9). It was as if he were arguing with a friend; at one moment he would appear to be feeling impatient, nodding his head energetically, then he would seem to be listening quietly, then you would see him disputing and struggling, and laughing and weeping all at once, fixing then lowering his gaze, then again speaking quietly and beating his breast. If anyone was inquisitive enough to want to spy on him secretly, he would find that the holy father Dominic was like Moses, who went into the innermost desert and saw the burning bush and the Lord speaking and calling to him to humble himself (Exod. 3:1ff). The man of God had a prophetic way of passing over quickly from reading to prayer and from meditation to contemplation.

When he was reading like this on his own, he used to ven-

Juliet Pannett

erate the book and bow to it and sometimes kiss it, particularly if it was a book of the gospels or if he was reading the words which Christ had spoken with his own lips. And sometimes he used to hide his face and turn it aside, or he would bury his face in his hands or hide it a little in his scapular. And then he would also become anxious and full of yearning, and he would also rise a little, respectfully, and bow as if he were thanking some very special person for favours received. Then, quite refreshed and at peace in himself, he would continue reading his book.

The ninth way of prayer

He also used to observe this way of prayer when he was going from one country to another, especially when he was in a lonely place. He disported himself with his meditations in his contemplation. And sometimes he would say to his travelling companions. 'It is written in Hosea, "I will lead her to a lonely

place and speak to her heart" ' (Hos. 2:14). So sometimes he went aside from his companion or went on ahead or, more likely, lingered far behind; going on on his own he would pray as he walked, and a fire was kindled in his meditation (Ps. 38:4).

A curious thing about this kind of prayer was that he seemed to be brushing away ashes or flies from his face, and because of this he often defended himself with the sign of the cross. The brethren thought that in this kind of prayer the saint acquired the fullness of sacred scripture and the very heart of the understanding of God's words, and also a power and boldness to preach fervently and a hidden intimacy with the Holy Spirit to know hidden things.

Thus it happened once, to mention just one story out of many which we omit, that the devil came to the church of the Friars Preachers in Bologna in the form of a young man of frivolous, licentious character and asked for someone to hear his confession. Five priests were brought to him, one after another. This was because the first confessor was so viciously disturbed and enflamed by his words that he got up from listening to his confession and refused to hear such dreadful things to the end. The second did the same and so did the third, fourth and fifth. But they went away without saying anything and they were not prepared to reveal this confession because, as far as they were concerned, what they had heard was a sacramental confession, even though it was the devil's. Then the sacristan approached St Dominic, who was in the priory at the time, complaining about these priests, because five of them had not been able to hear one sinner's confession. 'It's scandalous,' he added, 'the priests preach penance and then they refuse to give a penance to sinners.' Then the holy father Dominic got up from his reading and prayer and contemplation, not, I think, unaware of what was afoot, and went to hear the devil's confession. When he entered the church, the devil came to him and at once the holy father recognised him and said to him, 'You evil spirit, why do you tempt the servants of God under this veil of piety?' And he rebuked him severely. The devil disappeared at once, leaving the church reeking of sulphur. And the sacristan was appeased and stopped being angry with the priests.

THE POWER OF HIS PRAYER

(83)   The blessed father once received into the order someone from Apulia called Brother Thomas, whom he loved with a holy love because of his innocence and simplicity, so much so that the brethren called him St Dominic's son. One day some companions of his, real minions of the devil, seized the opportunity to drag him off by force and by deception into a certain vineyard, where they stripped him of his habit and clothed him in secular dress. When the brethren heard about it, they ran to the father and said, 'Look, your son is being dragged back

to the world by his friends.' At once the saint went into the church and prostrated himself in prayer, and not in vain. The results showed the power of his prayer. As soon as the shirt which they were putting on him touched Brother Thomas's skin he began to scream, 'Help! I am all on fire!' And he was unable to be quiet until the shirt was taken off him and he was reclothed in his religious habit and brought back to the cloister. Afterwards he lived a long time as a useful and very pleasing friar. [*Lives of the Brethren* II 11]

(84)   Once, when the father was travelling through France, he came to the town of Châtillon and it so happened that the son of the sister of the chaplain who had received him as a guest fell from the balcony. His mother and the rest of the family were weeping for him as if he were dead, but St Dominic, feeling sorry for them, prostrated himself in prayer, with tears, and God heard his prayer, so that he was able to restore the child alive and well to his mother. Thus their sadness was turned into joy and the boy's uncle invited many Godfearing people round to celebrate with a great banquet. But, while the others were eating eels, the boy's mother was unable to touch them because she was suffering from a quartan fever. So St Dominic made the sign of the cross over a little bit of eel and gave it to her in the name of Christ, saying, 'Eat it in the power of the Lord our Saviour.' She ate it and her fever was entirely cured. [Ibid. II 12]

(85)   When Bishop Alatrinus[3] was still prior of the Cistercian monastery of Casamari, he was on one occasion sent by Pope Honorius, of good memory, to Germany. When he was passing through Bologna, he went to visit his friend the man of God, Dominic, with whom he had become very intimate in Rome. At that time there was a master in Bologna, called Conrad the German, and the brethren felt an extraordinary desire that he should enter the order. So, on the vigil of the Assumption, the man of God Dominic was having a private and encouraging

conversation with the Cistercian prior, of whom he was very fond, about the things of God and the delights of heaven, when he confided to him, since the subject matter required it, 'I will admit to you, Father Prior, something I have never yet told anyone, and you must not tell anyone else as long as I am alive: never yet have I asked for anything in this life from God which I have not obtained just as I wished.' The prior was amazed at this. Being aware of the desire that the brethren had for the conversion of Master Conrad to religious life, he confidently added, 'If that is so, Father, ask God to give you Master Conrad for the order, whose entry the brethren are plainly clamouring for.' He replied, 'Good brother, it is a difficult thing you ask, but if you will apply yourself to prayer tonight with me, I trust in the Lord that he will not deprive us of the desire we are praying for.' So after compline, when the brethren went to bed, the man of God Dominic stayed in church, with his visitor present and watching, and he spent the night in prayer, as was his custom. After the solemn celebration of matins, as the day was dawning and the brethren were assembling for prime, just when the cantor began the hymn 'Now the daystar has arisen', suddenly Master Conrad arrived, who was truly to become a new daystar, and, prostrating himself at the feet of the blessed father Dominic, he urgently asked to be given the habit of the order, which he duly received and never looked back. [Constantine 58]

(86)   A certain dean from France, on his way to Rome, found the man of God Dominic preaching in Modena and went to him to discuss the salvation of his soul. In the course of the conversation he dolefully explained what he said would inevitably cause him to founder, namely that he could not resist sexual temptation. For this reason, as if his case were already desperate, he refrained from doing other good works too. The man of God comforted him with the divine confidence of which he was full. 'Go,' he said, 'in future be a man and do not despair of God's mercy. I will ask the Lord to give you chastity.'

His words were proved manifestly true by what followed. The man who had been impure and unchaste became chaste and self-controlled. The Lord had said, 'Truly I tell you, if you ask for anything from the Father in my name, he will give it to you' (John 16:23), and the promise of his servant was fully in line with this and with the Lord's purpose. [Ibid. 59]

Not only prayer and contemplation, but also the spiritual gifts with which Dominic was so richly endowed refined his natural intelligence and enabled him to view things, people and events, not only in their natural context, but also in the context of God's plan. His contemporaries interpreted his behaviour, which was often humanly inexplicable, as due to prophetic vision. His charisms awakened his latent talents for life and enabled them to become fruitful for other people and for the church of his time.

(87) Brother John of Spain said that, when he was with Brother Dominic in the community at Toulouse, Brother Dominic sent him, in spite of his reluctance, with five clerics and one laybrother to Paris, to study and preach and establish a community there, against the wishes of Count de Montfort and the archishop of Narbonne and the bishop of Toulouse and various other prelates. He told them not to worry, because everything would work out well for them. And he said to the prelates and the Count and the brethren, 'Do not gainsay me; I know quite well what I am doing.' Then he sent some others to Spain and gave them similar instructions and encouragement. While he, the witness, and his companions were studying in Paris, they were given the church of St Jacques, at the Porte d'Orléans, by Master John, the dean of St Quentin, who was teaching theology in Paris at the time, and by the university. There they settled and established a priory, where they received many good clerics into the Order of Friars Preachers. And they were given many properties and revenues at that time, and indeed everything worked out well for them, just as Brother Dominic had foretold. [Bologna Canonisation Process 26]

(88)   Invoking the Holy Spirit, Brother Dominic called the brethren together and told them that he had decided to send them out, few as they were, into all the world; he did not want them all to go on living together in Toulouse any longer. The announcement of this sudden dispersal amazed them, but their confidence in the evident authority which his sanctity gave him made them more prepared to agree to what he said, because they were hopeful that it would all lead to a satisfactory outcome. [Jordan, *Libellus* 47]

(89)   Another thing that must not be passed over in silence is how the man of God was not unaware of the death of Count de Montfort, thanks to a mysterious vision in which the power of God revealed it to him. While he was asleep he had an imaginary vision which was by no means devoid of meaning: he saw a tall tree, with widely spreading branches, lovely to look at because of the beauty of its thick foliage; a large number of birds were resting in its branches. But after a short while the tree fell down and the whole crowd of birds was scattered and flew away. At once, filled with the Spirit of God, he understood that Count de Montfort, who was a great prince and protector of those who needed protection, was shortly to be cut off in death. And this is exactly what happened in the outcome. [Constantine 57]

(90)   One Lent the man of God was living at Carcassonne in the bishop's house, devoting himself to preaching; he was also vicar general in spiritual matters, since the bishop was at that time in northern France. In those days there was a sharp increase in hostilities between Count Simon de Montfort, on the church's side, and the Count of Toulouse, and the Count of Toulouse was beginning to have a considerable advantage over the church. A Cistercian laybrother who was there was greatly distressed by all this and went to the man of God, Dominic, one day in his distress and said to him, 'Master Dominic, will these troubles never have an end?' The man of

111

God was silent, but the brother insisted all the more on his question, knowing that the Lord revealed many things to him, so at last, in the presence of Brother Stephen of Metz, who was his companion at the time and who also later spread the story around widely, he said, 'Certainly the wickedness of these people of Toulouse will have an end, it will have an end; but the end is far off, and in the mean time the blood of many will be shed, and a king will succumb and be killed in the conflict of this war.' His hearers were afraid that he was referring to the King of France, who had recently taken the Albigensian business in hand, but he said, 'Do not worry about the King of France, it is another king I mean whose life will be cut off and cut off soon by the changing fortunes of this present war.' The following year the King of Aragon fell in battle, supporting the side of the Count of Toulouse. Would that he had not fallen wretchedly forever by fighting against the church! [Ibid. 55]

(91)   When the man of God, Dominic, was in Rome and was praying in the basilica of St Peter's in the sight of God for the preservation and increase of the order which God's right hand was fostering through him, the hand of the Lord came upon him and he suddenly had a vision in his imagination in which he saw the great princes of the church, Peter and Paul, coming towards him. Peter seemed to hand him a staff and Paul a book, and they said to him, 'Go and preach, because you have been chosen for this ministry by God.' At once, in a moment of time, he seemed to see his sons scattered throughout the whole world, going two by two and preaching the word of God to the peoples. [Ibid. 25]

(92)   It was one of the most remarkable things about the servant of God, Master Dominic, that, when he sent the brethren hither and thither throughout the various parts of God's church, he always did so with complete confidence; he never hesitated or wavered, even though other people sometimes disagreed with what he was doing. It was as if he knew

exactly what was going to happen, or as if he had been given instructions by the Spirit in some revelation. And who would venture to say that it was not indeed so? At first he had only a few friars, and for the most part they were simple, uneducated men; yet he divided them up and scattered them throughout the church in such a way that, in the judgement of worldly prudence, he must have seemed to be destroying what he had begun rather than laying the foundation for something even greater. But he backed up everyone he sent out with his prayers, and the power of the Lord was with them to give them increase. [Jordan, *Libellus* 62]

(93)   In Florence there was a woman recently converted from the world to God by the man of God, Dominic. Her name was Bene, though she is now called Sister Benedicta. A cleric by the name of Hugh tormented her a lot. After she had many times complained about this in great distress to the man of God, Dominic, he finally comforted her gently with the words, 'Bear up patiently, my daughter, knowing that this man who is persecuting you and the order with such insolence will soon become a good friar in the order and there he will endure much hard work for a long time.' His word was reliable, as the outcome showed, following exactly what the man of God had predicted. [Constantine 52]

(94)   Brother Stephen said that, while he was studying in Bologna, Master Dominic came to Bologna and preached to the students and to other good people, and he, the witness, went to confession to him and got the impression that Master Dominic loved him. One evening when he, the witness, was going to have dinner in his hostel with his companions, Brother Dominic sent two friars to say to him, 'Brother Dominic bids you come to him at once.' He replied, 'As soon as I have had my dinner, I will come to him.' But they said, 'No, you are to come at once.' So he got up, left his companions and went to him. He found him at the church of St Nicholas with many

113

of the brethren. Brother Dominic said to the brethren, 'Teach him how to make a venia. [A ritual prostration used in religious life as a gesture of apology or supplication.]' The witness made a venia and then placed himself in Brother Dominic's hands and, before he left, he clothed him in the habit of the Friars Preachers saying, 'I want to give you weapons with which you are to fight the devil for the whole of your life.' He, the witness, was amazed at the time and afterwards, wondering what had prompted Brother Dominic to send for him like this and clothe him in the habit of the Friars Preachers, since he had never discussed becoming a religious with him. He believes that he did it because of some divine inspiration or revelation.

[Bologna Canonisation Process 36]

(95)   An elderly and very devout citizen of Bologna used often to relate to the brethren and to seculars that, when he was a young man, he had great devotion to St Dominic, who was at that time staying at Bologna. One day St Dominic was due to go and preach in some church in the city. Although the blessed father was a Spaniard, the people there understood every word he said clearly and without difficulty. Because of his outstanding holiness and the attractive and beneficial words he was given to speak by the grace of Christ, the people of Bologna listened to him avidly and, when they knew he was due to go somewhere to preach, they did not go ahead of him in the usual way to the place where he was going to preach, instead they all went first to the church of St Nicholas, where St Dominic lived with the brethren, and met him there with wonderful devotion and escorted him reverently to the place where he was due to preach. So when the narrator of this story had gone, with everyone else, to the church of St Nicholas to meet the blessed father, two students approached St Dominic and, as he himself could see and hear, one of them said to him, 'Please, Father, pray for me to the Lord to forgive my sins; I think that I am sorry for my offences and I have confessed all the sins I could remember.' St Dominic went to the altar and

made a brief prayer. Then he went back to the student and said to him, 'Trust in the Lord and persevere in love of him, because he has forgiven all your sins.' When the other student, the companion of the first, heard this, he said, 'Please, Father, pray for me also, since I too have confessed my sins.' St Dominic went back to the altar and made a brief prayer. Then he said to him, 'My son, do not be so foolish as to mock God, to your own harm; the confession you made of your sins was incomplete. Because you were embarrassed, there was one sin you did not mention.' Taking him to one side he revealed to him the sin he had been too ashamed to confess. He said, 'Forgive me, Father, it is all just as you have said.' When he had done all that was necessary for the student's guidance, he set off for the place appointed for his sermon, with all the people escorting him. [Berengarian Miracles 4]

(96)   Once, when the blessed father was travelling from Toulouse to Paris, he broke the journey at Rocamadour, where he spent the night devoutly in the church of Our Lady. The companion of his journey and of his holiness and devotion was Brother Bertrand, who was the first provincial of Province. The next day they met some German pilgrims on the road, who attached themselves to them devoutly, when they heard them reciting psalms and litanies. When they reached a town, the pilgrims invited the friars to join them and looked after them with characteristic generosity. This happened for four successive days. So one day St Dominic said to Brother Bertrand in distress, 'Brother Bertrand, it is really on my conscience that we have been reaping material benefits from these pilgrims, without sowing any spiritual seed in them. So, if you do not mind, let us kneel down and pray to the Lord and ask him to give us the ability both to understand and to speak their language, so that we can proclaim the Lord Jesus to them.' Having done this, to the amazement of the pilgrims, they both spoke German quite intelligibly. So for another four days they walked with them and spoke about the Lord Jesus until they reached

Orléans. Since the Germans wanted to go to Chartres, they left them on the Paris road, humbly commending themselves to the prayers of the friars. The next day the blessed father said to Brother Bertrand, 'Look, brother, we are going to Paris and, if the brethren hear of the miracle which the Lord has worked for us, they will think we are saints, when we are really sinners, and if it reaches the ears of people in the world, we shall be exposed to a great deal of vanity. So I command you under obedience not to tell anyone of what has happened until I am dead.' And so it was done. After the death of the blessed father Brother Bertrand told the whole story to devout brethren.

[*Lives of the Brethren* II 10]

For Dominic, as for the people of the Old Testament and the Middle Ages, the gospel of salvation was not confined to the mind and the soul, it extended to the entire reality of human life, including the body and society and everything that oppresses and threatens people. As was the case with Jesus, Dominic's contemporaries saw some of his actions as miraculous and considered him to be a wonder-worker. The people of that time found it easier than we do today to believe in miracles, especially as the 'apostolic life' took seriously the charge of Jesus, not only to preach the kingdom of God, but also to drive out demons and heal the sick (Mark 3:15; 6:7, 13). Dominic lived so totally for the preaching of the kingdom that it is entirely credible that his word was accompanied also by these other phenomena, which Jesus' message of salvation for the whole human person foretold.

(97)   An elderly and respectable citizen of Cahors told the brethren, and said he was prepared to swear to it, something that he saw in person when he was at the siege of Toulouse with Count de Montfort. Some pilgrims from England who were on their way to Santiago did not want to go into Toulouse because the place had been excommunicated, so they boarded a small boat to cross the river. Because of their number (there were about forty of them) the boat sank and they all fell into

the river, so that not even their heads could be seen above water. The shouts of the drowning men and of the army which was nearby roused St Dominic, who was praying in a church by the river, so he came out and, when he saw their danger, he prostrated himself, stretching out his arms in the shape of a cross, and cried out to God, weeping bitterly, to deliver his pilgrims from death. Standing up again after a little while, filled with confidence in God, he commanded the pilgrims in the name of Christ to come to the bank. Then an extraordinary thing happened, but it was done by him 'who alone works marvels' (Ps. 71:18): immediately, in the sight of everyone who had come to see this tragic spectacle, the pilgrims appeared above the surface of the water. The people ran up on all sides and held out lances and spears to them and brought them all safely out of the river. [*Lives of the Brethren* II 3]

(98)   St Dominic used often to travel round the territory of Toulouse to preach and it happened once that, while he was fording a little stream called the Ariège, some books he was carrying in a fold of his habit fell out in the middle of the stream, as he was tucking up his clothes. Praising God, he came to the house of a certain good lady and he told her about the loss of his books. Three days later a fisherman cast his line into the water in the same place and, expecting to land a fish, he brought up St Dominic's books, which were as unharmed as if they had been kept in a cupboard with the utmost care, which was all the more remarkable in that they had no cloth or leather binding or anything at all to protect them. The good lady received the books and sent them on to the blessed father in Toulouse with great joy. [Ibid. II 4]

(99)   One day, when he was travelling round preaching the gospel in the territory of Toulouse, the man of God, Dominic, with many others, crossed a stretch of water in a ferry and the boatman who had ferried them insisted on getting a denier from him as his fare. The man of God promised him the

kingdom of heaven in return for his services, adding that he was a servant and disciple of Christ and did not carry any gold or silver with him (Matt. 10:9). The boatman, far from being impressed by this promise, was rather provoked by it to insist all the more on getting his fare. Seizing him by his cappa he said, 'Either you leave me this cappa or you pay me a denier.' The man of God raised his eyes to heaven and prayed for a while in himself; then he looked at the ground and saw a denier lying there, which was no doubt supplied by the will of God. 'There, brother,' he said, 'take what you are demanding and leave me in peace.' [Constantine 43]

(100)   One day he was travelling with many others in those parts and at lunchtime they had nothing but a beaker of wine. The blessed father felt sorry for some of the brethren, who had been used to a high standard of living in the world, so he ordered the little wine they had to be poured into a big jug together with a lot of water. There were eight brethren in all, and they all had plenty to drink of the water which had turned into wine – indeed there was more there than they needed.

[*Lives of the Brethren* II 5]

(101) After this the glorious father returned to Italy, accompanied by a laybrother called John. While they were crossing the Alps in Lombardy, Brother John suddenly began to fail from hunger, so that he could not go on or even get up from the ground, he was so worn out. The merciful father said to him, 'What's the matter, my son? Why can't you go on?' He said, 'Holy father, I am overwhelmed by hunger.' The saint replied, 'Be strong, my son, let us go on a little further, then we shall come to a place where we can find something to eat.' Brother John insisted that he really could not go on at all, but was on the verge of collapsing entirely. So the holy man, moved by the mercy in which he abounded and by the brother's plight, turned to his usual resort and prayed briefly to the Lord. Then, turning to the brother, he said, 'Get up, my son, and go over

there and bring back whatever you find there.' The brother just managed to get up and went as best he could to the place indicated by the saint, which was about a stone's throw away. When he got there, he found a single loaf of astonishing whiteness, wrapped up in the whitest of cloths. He picked it up and took it back to the holy man of God, who told him to eat a little of it. He did so and it gave him all the strength he needed. Asked by the man of God whether his hunger had gone so that he would be able to continue the journey, he replied that he was sufficiently refreshed and was well able to continue, even though before he had not been able to move. 'So,' the saint said, 'get up, my son, and wrap the rest of the loaf up again and put it back where you found it.' When he had done this, they resumed their journey. When they had gone a little way, the brother realised what had happened and said to himself, 'My God, who put that bread there and where did it come from? What a dolt I am not to have paid attention and investigated!' Then he said to the saint, 'Holy father, that bread we found – where did it come from and who put it there?' St Dominic, true lover and keeper of humility that he was, asked him, 'My son, did you eat all you needed?' He said, 'Yes.' 'Well then,' the saint went on, 'if you have eaten enough, give thanks to God, as is fitting, and do not ask any more questions.' Brother John, to whom this happened, later returned to Spain and told the brethren all about it. Eventually he was sent with the brethren who went to Africa at the pope's command to preach the Catholic faith and there he died in Morocco, having happily run his course. [Ibid. II 8]

(102) Brother Reginald, the pope's penitentiary and later archbishop of Armagh, a very religious man, reported that he was present in Bologna when the procurator went to the man of God, Dominic, and began to complain that he had nothing to put before the huge number of friars except two loaves of bread. That imitator of the Lord, Dominic, ordered them to be broken up into small pieces. Then, trusting in the Lord 'who

is rich towards all who call upon him' (Rom. 10:12) and who 'fills every living thing with his blessing' (Ps. 144:16), he pronounced the blessing and made the server go round the tables placing two or three morsels of bread in each place. When the server had gone round once, there was still some bread left, so he went round again, and then a third time, putting a little of the bread in each place, and still there was plenty left of that small supply. To cut a long story short, he went round so often giving bread to the brethren that they all had ample and much more bread was taken up again at the end of the meal, by God's gift, than had been supplied in the first place by men. [Ibid. II 20]

(103)   In San Sisto an architect employed by the brethren was crushed when a crypt collapsed on him and he lay buried for a long time under the pile of fallen material, quite dead. The brethren came running at this unexpected disaster, saddened beyond measure. They were worried both by the uncertainty of the dead man's state of soul and by the risk that the people would turn against them because of what had happened among them. The position of the order was not yet well known, so their reputation could easily be damaged. But the merciful father, the man of God, Dominic, whose heart was confident in the Lord (Daniel 13:35), could not endure the anguish of his sons, so he ordered the body of the dead man to be brought up from the crypt and by his prayers he immediately restored him both to life and to health. [Constantine 36]

◦ 7 ◦

SPEAKING OF GOD

'God had given him a special grace to weep for sinners, for the distressed, for the afflicted; he bore their troubles in the inmost shrine of his compassion . . .' (Jordan, *Libellus* 12). The strength of Dominic's compassion was rooted in his charity; it was not a superficial effervescence of emotion. It was charity that made him act compassionately. His compassion, upheld by charity, did not look down on the needy and the less powerful, it raised them up to himself, so that the weak and the suffering became his partners. Even as a student in Palencia Dominic felt so moved by the plight of the starving that he sold his books and all that he possessed and established a charitable foundation for the poor, with the words, 'I refuse to study on dead skins, while people are dying of hunger' (Bologna Canonisation Process 35). But it was not only the poor and the hungry that he embraced. He encountered yet another lack which challenged him to action: lack of the faith. He met it first in Languedoc, more or less by chance, in the form of the dualistic heresy of the Cathars. Soon afterwards it confronted him in northern Germany, where he got to know the pagan tribe of the Cumans. This encounter persuaded him to do his utmost for his brothers and sisters who lacked the faith. That was his way into the world.

His resolve matured in prayer. Dominic had asked God to 'grant him true charity, which would be effective in caring for and obtaining the salvation of other people' (Jordan, *Libellus* 13). Charity alone enabled him to be completely at God's disposal and to lose his life in order to toil for the salvation of his brothers and sisters. Only in this light can we understand the numerous texts which speak of his zeal for the salvation of everybody and of his compassion for people suffering from the egoism and injustice of others, as well as for people whose faith was imperilled by beguilement or ignorance.

121

Because merciful, compassionate love is unwilling to remain alone, Dominic endeavoured to awaken this same love in his brethren. Through the preaching of the word of God they were to disclose to the world new sources of salvation.

(104)   Brother Ventura said that [Dominic] was so zealous for souls that he extended his charity and his compassion, not only to the faithful, but also to pagans and unbelievers and even the damned in hell, and he wept a great deal for them. He was very enthusiastic both to preach himself and to send out others as preachers, to such an extent that he wanted to go and preach to the pagans. [Bologna Canonisation Process 11]

(105)   Brother William of Monferrato said that [Dominic] seemed more zealous for the salvation of the human race than anyone he had ever seen. In the same year in which he met Brother Dominic he, the witness, went to Paris to study theology, because he had first promised and made an arrangement with Brother Dominic that, after he had studied theology for two years and after Brother Dominic had organised his order, they would both go together and convert the pagans living in Prussia and in other northern lands. [Ibid. 12]

(106)   Brother Rudolph said that he had never seen anyone whose religion and devotion pleased him so much as Brother Dominic. He also said that he yearned for the salvation of the souls of everyone, including even Saracens as well as Christians, and particularly the Cumans and others. He was more zealous for souls than anyone he, the witness, had ever seen. He often said that he longed to go to the Cumans and other unbelieving tribes. [Ibid. 32]

(107)   Brother Paul of Venice said that [Dominic] greatly desired the salvation of the souls of believers and unbelievers alike. And he often said to the witness, 'Once we have organised and established our order, we shall go to the Cumans

and preach the faith of Christ to them and win them for the Lord'. [Ibid. 43]

(108)   Brother Frugerio said that [Dominic] was very zealous for the salvation of souls, not only of Christians, but also of Saracens and other unbelievers, and he encouraged the brethren to be similarly zealous. His zeal for the salvation of souls was such that he had decided, once he had organised his friars, to go to the pagans and, if need be, to die for the faith. Asked how he knows this, the witness replied that he had seen him speaking and acting like this. [Ibid. 47]

The desire to go to the pagans as a missionary, which had been awakened in Dominic at his encounter with the Cumans in northern Germany, never left him until his death. Providence, however, had appointed another mission for him, among the heretics in the south of France. Even on his first journey to northern Germany with Bishop Diego in 1203 he encountered one such heretic in Toulouse.

(109)   When Bishop Diego learned that the people in that neighbourhood had been heretics for some time, he was sincerely upset and sorry for all the many souls who were being so wretchedly deceived. During the night which they spent in lodgings in Toulouse, the subprior [Dominic] argued powerfully and passionately with their host, who was a heretic, and at last brought him back to the faith by the help of the Spirit of God, because the heretic 'was unable to withstand the wisdom and Spirit which was addressing him' (Acts 6:10).

[Jordan, *Libellus* 15]

The encounter with the Cumans during the second trip to northern Germany in 1205–1206 was a real shock for Bishop Diego and Dominic. As a result of it they decided to go to Rome to beg the pope's permission to go as missionaries to this wild pagan people.

(110)   The bishop sent a messenger back to the king and then made use of the opportunity to hurry off with his clergy to the papal court. When he came into the presence of Pope Innocent, he urgently begged to be allowed to resign his see, if possible, pleading, from many points of view, his own incompetence and arguing that the enormous dignity of his office was beyond his powers. He also opened his mind to the pope about a purpose he had conceived of devoting all his energies to the conversion of the Cumans, should the pope allow his resignation. But the pope refused and would not even accept his request to be allowed, or commanded as an act of penance for his sins, to go to the territory of the Cumans to preach, while remaining a bishop. This was, of course, due to a hidden purpose of God, who had destined the energies of this great man for a rich harvest of salvation in another direction. [Jordan, *Libellus* 17]

They were thus obliged to return home. On their way, they met the papal legates at Montpellier, who had been toiling over the heretics with no success. Bishop Diego and Dominic gave them advice about how they should proceed, and they took the lead by setting an example of what should be done. Thus began a new style of missionary activity. At this stage Dominic is still only the faithful follower and friend of his bishop, but, as the years go by, he emerges as the heir of Diego's vision and as the providential instrument for its realisation and development into something much bigger. An account of the beginning of the mission in the south of France is given by the Cistercian, Pierre des Vaux-de-Cernai, who was himself present for much of the time.

(111)   When he was at Montpellier, on his way home from the curia, the bishop of Osma met there the venerable Arnaud, abbot of Cîteaux, and Brother Peter of Castelnau and Brother Raoul, all of them Cistercian monks; these were the pope's legates but, depressed by their inability to make any significant headway in their preaching to the heretics, they were thinking of abandoning their mission. Whenever they wanted to preach

to the heretics, the heretics brought up against them the objection of the appalling lives of the clergy. But if they were to try to reform the lives of the clergy, they would have to give up their preaching. [Pierre des Vaux-de-Cernai 20]

(112)   In face of this dilemma, Bishop Diego gave them the sound advice that they should forget about everything else and devote themselves even more earnestly to preaching; and, to enable them to shut the mouths of their malicious enemies, they should proceed in humility, like their loving Master, 'doing and teaching' (Acts 1:1), travelling on foot, without gold or silver, imitating in every way the pattern of the apostles. The legates were reluctant to adopt such a novel policy on their own, but said that if someone of suitable authority were to give them a lead in pursuing this way, they would gladly follow. Without hesitating, the God-filled bishop offered himself and at once sent his retinue and his carriages back to his own town of Osma and set off from Montpellier with only one companion [Dominic], together with two of the Cistercians, Peter and Raoul. The abbot of Cîteaux went back to Cîteaux because the General Chapter of their order was soon to be held there, and because he intended, after the Chapter, to bring some of the abbots of his order to help him in carrying out the task of preaching which had been laid upon him. [Ibid. 21]

(113)   [The legates] listened to Bishop Diego's advice and, inspired by his example, they agreed to adopt a similar policy themselves. They sent back to their monasteries everything that they had brought with them, except for the books which they would need for the celebration of the Office and for study and, should the opportunity arise, for purposes of debate. They accepted the bishop as their superior and as the head of the whole enterprise and set off on foot and without provisions, to proclaim the faith in voluntary poverty. When the heretics saw this, they launched a counter-offensive of more insistent preaching. [Jordan, *Libellus* 22]

(114)   Bishop Diego kept with him Dominic, his subprior, for whom he had a high regard and a warm affection. This Dominic was the first founder and the first member of the Order of Preachers, and from that time onwards he was no longer called 'subprior' but 'Brother Dominic'. And 'Dominic' indeed he was, because he was kept by the Lord (*custoditus a domino*) innocent of sin and because he kept the Lord's will (*domini custodiens voluntatem*) with all his might. [Ibid. 21]

According to some of the first Dominicans to join the order in the south of France, Bishop Diego had already discovered for himself the problem facing the legates. The advice which he gave them was based on his own humiliating experience and, as the Dominicans realised in retrospect, it not merely transformed the papal mission against the heretics, it sowed the seed from which the Order of Preachers grew.

(115)   When Diego, bishop of Osma, had come into the land of the Albigensians with his episcopal baggage train and horses, and learned that the district was infected with heresy, he preached in one of the towns there against heresy. The heretics rose up to oppose him, and the strongest argument they could find to support their false beliefs was the pomp of the bishop's équipe. 'How can you believe this man and his like?', they said to their adherents. 'They turn up with all this pomp and wealth, with their pack-animals and their riding-horses, and then they preach to you a Christ who was humble and poor. We, by contrast, preach in poverty and lowliness and austerity, we display in our deeds what we have told you about in our words.' This embarrassed the bishop, so he sent away his horses and his équipe and abandoned his provisions and began to go round the district with St Dominic in poverty and on foot, preaching. This was the reason why our order was founded. I was told about this by the first brethren who were with St Dominic in that country. [Stephen of Bourbon 83]

(116)   Setting off from Montpellier, the bishop of Osma and the two monks came to a town called Servian, where they found a leader of the heretics, called Baldwin, and a certain Thierry, a son of perdition and stubble for eternal burning. He was originally from northern France, a nobleman by birth and had been a canon of Nevers. When his uncle, who was a knight and a dreadful heretic, was condemned for heresy at a Council of Paris in the presence of the papal legate, Cardinal Octavian, this Thierry saw that he could no longer remain undetected, so he moved to the neighbourhood of Narbonne. There he was held in the utmost love and respect by the heretics, both because he seemed to be rather more acute than the rest and because they were proud to have someone from the kingdom of France, where the fount of science and of the Christian religion is acknowledged to be, as an associate in their belief and a defender of their crime. Nor should it be overlooked that he had himself called 'Thierry', though previously he was called William. [Pierre des Vaux-de-Cernai 22]

(117)   Our preachers debated with Baldwin and Thierry for eight days and their profitable counsel converted all the people of the town to hate the heretics, so that they would gladly have expelled the heretics from their midst, only the lord of the town, who was himself tainted with the poison of infidelity, had accepted them as his intimate friends. It would take too long to report the whole debate in detail, but I think it is worth mentioning one thing: when the venerable bishop's arguments had reduced him to complete helplessness, Thierry commented, 'I know of what spirit you are: you have come in the spirit of Elijah' (Luke 1:17). To this the holy man replied, 'If I have come in the spirit of Elijah, you have come in the spirit of the antichrist.' When the preachers left the town at the end of the eight days, the people escorted them for more than a mile. [Ibid. 23]

(118)   Going straight on, the preachers came to the city of

Béziers, where they debated and preached for fifteen days, strengthening the few Catholics there in their faith and confounding the heretics. But the venerable bishop of Osma and Brother Raoul advised Brother Peter of Castelnau to leave them for a time, because they were afraid that he would be killed, as he was hated by the heretics more than anyone else. So Brother Peter withdrew from them for a time, but the others left Béziers and came without mishap to Carcassonne, where they stayed for eight days, devoting themselves to preaching and debates. [Ibid. 24]

(119)   One of the first meetings was at Verfeil, at which many leaders of the heretics were present, including Pons Jourda and Arnaud Arrufat. Many points were raised on both sides, and then they turned their attention to the Lord's saying in John 3:13, 'No one goes up into heaven except the one who came down from heaven.' The bishop of Osma asked how they understood this saying. One of them replied that Jesus, who uttered this saying, was calling himself 'son of the man who is in heaven'.[1] 'So,' the bishop said, 'it is your view that his Father, who is in heaven, is a man and that he is calling himself the son of this man?' They agreed that this was their view. Then the bishop said, 'So, since the Lord says, through Isaiah, "Heaven is my throne and earth my footstool" (Is. 66:1), it follows that, if he is a man sitting in heaven, with his feet touching the earth, the distance between heaven and earth is the length of his legs.' They admitted that they supposed this to be so. He at once went on, 'May God curse you for being gross heretics! I thought you would have had something more subtle than that.' They took refuge in other texts, seeking somewhere to hide, for the Catholics used the text cited to prove that Christ is God and man, who came down from heaven to become man and is nevertheless, as God, in heaven from where he came down. Other heretics too were shown up, as even people who were hostile to the church concluded. I once heard Bishop Fulk mention something that a sensible knight, Pons

Adémar de Roudeille, had said to him at the time: 'We would never have been able to believe that Rome had so many effective arguments against these people.' [Puylaurens 8]

(120) It would be tedious to relate in detail how those apostolic men, our preachers, went round the towns, preaching and debating everywhere, so let us proceed straight to the most important things. One day all the leaders of the heretics assembled in a town in the diocese of Carcassonne called Montréal, to debate with one accord against our preachers. Brother Peter of Castelnau returned for this debate (he had, you remember, left his companions at Béziers). Judges were appointed for the debate from among the Catharist believers. The debate went on for fifteen days and the arguments on both sides were written down and given to the judges, for them to pronounce a final verdict. They saw that their heretics had been manifestly defeated, so they refused to give a verdict. They would not even return the papers they had received from our side, for fear that they would be made public; instead they gave them to the heretics. [Pierre des Vaux-de-Cernai 26]

(121) At this time a miracle occurred, which it is worth inserting here. Those religious men, our preachers, had been debating one day with the heretics, and one of our people, called Dominic, a completely holy man who had been the companion of the bishop of Osma, put down in writing the texts he had cited and handed the paper over to one of the heretics, for him to think about the points raised. That night the heretics were assembled in some house, sitting by the fire. The one to whom the man of God had given the paper brought it out into the open. Then his companions told him to throw it into the middle of the fire; if it burned up, the faith (or unfaith) of the heretics would be true, but if it remained unburned, they would admit that the faith preached by our side was good. They all agreed to this, so the paper was thrown into the fire. After staying in the fire for a short time, it leaped

out again, completely unburned. The people who were there were amazed, but one, who was more hardened than the rest, said, 'Throw the paper in the fire again and then we shall have fuller evidence of the truth.' So it was thrown back into the fire and again it leaped out unburned. Seeing this, that hard man, slow to believe (Luke 24:25), said, 'Throw it in a third time – then we shall know the outcome without any doubt.' It was thrown into the fire for the third time and again it did not burn, but leaped out entirely unharmed by the fire. Even after seeing so many signs, the heretics refused to be converted to the faith; continuing in their hardness, they strictly bound each other never to tell anyone about this miracle, in case it should come to the knowledge of our side. But a knight who was there with them, who was to some extent sympathetic to our faith, was unwilling to conceal what he had seen and told several people about it. All this happened at Montréal, as I heard from the outstanding religious who had given the paper to the heretic. [Ibid. 54]

From the time when he became involved in the mission in the south of France until his death Bishop Diego shuttled between Spain and Languedoc, as the researches of Jarl Gallén have shown. This is why Pierre des Vaux-de-Cernai quite correctly says that Dominic 'had been his companion' (121). However much he valued his companionship, the bishop appreciated that Dominic was needed in the mission against the heretics. The Dominicans retained no memory of Diego's trips to Spain, so their writings give the misleading impression that he stayed in France for the whole time. They also forgot that, until 1215 or so, Dominic was not officially in charge of the papal mission. After the loss of the original three legates, abbot Guy of Vaux-de-Cernai was the head of the mission, as we learn from his nephew, Pierre. Guy later became Bishop of Carcassonne, where Dominic was for a time his vicar general.[2]

(122) Bishop Diego exercised his ministry of preaching for two years, but at the end of this time he decided to return to

Spain, to avoid incurring the charge of neglecting his own church of Osma if he stayed away any longer. After visiting his church he intended to come back, bringing some money with him to finish building his monastery for sisters; he also wanted, with the pope's consent, to appoint men in that region who would be suitable as preachers, whose task it would be to keep on hammering away at the errors of the heretics and tirelessly to support the truth of the faith. [Jordan, *Libellus* 28]

(123) He left Brother Dominic in charge of the spiritual goverment of those who remained behind, because he knew him to be a man genuinely full of the Spirit. In temporal affairs William Claret of Pamiers was to be in charge, it being understood that he was to give an account to Brother Dominic of everything he did. [Ibid. 29]

(124) So the bishop took leave of the brethren and set off on foot. After passing through Castile he arrived at Osma. But a few days later he fell ill and finished his life in this world in great sanctity, winning a glorious reward for the good and hard work he had done, going to his grave in prosperity (Job 5:26) to enter into a wealthy rest (Is. 32:18). It is said that after his death he also won renown for working miracles, and it would not be surprising if he were powerful in this way in the presence of God, since even while he was among men in this weak and miserable dwelling place of ours his life was characterised by remarkable evidence of God's favours and by the resplendent beauty of his virtues. [Ibid. 30]

(125) When news of the death of the man of God reached the missionaries who had stayed on in the Toulouse district, they all went back to their homes. Brother Dominic was the only one who carried on preaching the whole time. Some people did join him for a time, but they were not bound to him by any promise of obedience. Among those who joined him were William Claret, whom we have already met, and a

Spaniard called Brother Dominic, who was later the prior of Madrid in Spain. [Ibid. 31]

(126)   Before Bishop Diego died, that man of happy memory, Brother Raoul, had also succumbed to his fate and died in a Cistercian monastery near Saint-Gilles, called Franquevaux. With these two luminaries gone, namely the bishop of Osma and Brother Raoul, the venerable abbot Guy of Vaux-de-Cernai in the diocese of Paris was appointed prior and master of the preachers. He had come with the other abbots to the province of Narbonne in order to preach. He was noble by birth, but nobler far in his knowledge and virtue. Later he became bishop of Carcassonne. The abbot of Cîteaux had taken himself off elsewhere, being busy at the time with certain great matters. So the holy preachers traipsed around, manifestly showing up the heretics in their debates with them, though they were unable to convert them because of their obstinate ill-will. Quite a long time later they returned to northern France, seeing that they could achieve little or nothing by their preaching and debating. One thing which must not be passed over is that, after the abbot of Vaux-de-Cernai had debated several times with Thierry and another important leader of the heretics, Bernard of Simorre, who was considered their most prominent man in Carcassonne, and after he had frequently shown up their errors, Thierry one day said to the abbot, having no more answers to give him, 'For a long time I was held in the clutches of the whore, but she shall never hold me again' (meaning by 'the whore' the Roman church). Another thing too is worth mentioning: one day the abbot of Vaux-de-Cernai went to a town near Carcassonne called Laure to preach there and, as he entered the town, he made the sign of the cross. A heretical knight who was in the town saw him do it and remarked to the abbot, 'May I never be helped by the sign of the cross!' [Pierre des Vaux-de-Cernai 50–53].

Even the pope, Innocent III, changed his opinion about how

to fight heresy and confirmed the new way of preaching, which had been adopted from the very people who were to be converted. He ordered his legate, Raoul of Fontfroide, to appoint preachers to the heretics in the province of Narbonne, on the authority of the pope, to win them back to the truth by word and example.

(127)   We are consumed with zeal for his house (Ps. 68:10), who has granted it to us, unworthy though we are, to sit on the high watchtower, and we desire to be weak with the weak (1 Cor. 9:22) and to apply fatherly counsel, whereby wounds may be treated and even the swollen sore (Is. 1:6) be tended, as far as in us lies. We therefore command and instruct you, by these apostolic letters, to find tested men, whom you see to be apt for the task, who are not afraid to go to the despised, imitating the poverty of Christ in degrading clothes and in an ardent spirit; enjoin upon them, in remission of their sins, to hasten to the heretics to call them back from their errors, by God's grace, through the example of their deeds and the teaching of their words. [Innocent III, Letter of 17 November 1206]

After the death of Bishop Diego on 30 December 1207 the Cistercian monks returned to their abbeys and the mission practically came to an end. On 14 January 1208 the papal legate, Peter of Castelnau, was murdered, whereupon Innocent III reiterated with great urgency his call for a crusade; the result was one of the most cruel religious wars in history. Dominic, however, remained in the area with a few faithful followers and continued his peaceful mission.

(128)   While the crusaders were in the land, Brother Dominic remained there until the death of the Count de Montfort, constantly preaching the word of God. [Jordan, *Libellus* 34]

(129)   Count de Montfort was particularly devoted to him; with his men's consent he gave an important estate called Casseneuil to him and his followers and to those who were helping him in the mission of salvation which had been started

there. In addition Brother Dominic held the church of Fanjeaux and certain other properties, from which he could provide for the needs of himself and his associates. The Order of Preachers had not yet been founded and they had done no more than discuss such a foundation, although Brother Dominic was already applying himself with all his might to the task of preaching; nor were they yet observing the constitution which was later promulgated about not accepting properties and not keeping properties which had been accepted previously. In this way about ten years passed from the death of the bishop of Osma up to the Lateran Council, and all this time Brother Dominic remained there more or less alone. [Ibid. 37]

Dominic remained almost eight years in the area, under the most difficult circumstances, working for reconciliation and moderation. But he soon saw that his own energies were insufficient for the accomplishment of this enormous task. Therefore he made up his mind to establish an order. This probably happened on Easter Day, 19 April 1215.

(130)   At the time when the bishops were beginning to go to Rome for the Lateran Council, two upright and suitable men from Toulouse gave themselves to Christ's servant, Dominic. One of them was Peter Seilhan, who was later prior of Limoges, the other was Brother Thomas, a very attractive and eloquent man. Brother Peter made over to Brother Dominic and his companions some tall, noble houses which he possessed in Toulouse near the Château Narbonnais, and it was in these houses that the brethren now first began to live in Toulouse, and from that time onwards all those who were with Brother Dominic began to humble themselves more and more profoundly and to adopt the manner of religious. [Ibid. 38]

What Dominic had practised and lived for eight years was now given institutional form. It was his personal ideal which guided his life: itinerant preaching combined with mendicancy, though this last was for the time being mitigated by some fixed income. Bishop Fulk of Toulouse confirmed this ideal in June or July 1215.

(131)   In the name of our Lord Jesus Christ. Let all men know, now and in the time to come, that we, Fulk, humble servant by God's grace of the see of Toulouse, hereby appoint as preachers in our diocese Brother Dominic and his companions, to root out the evil of heresy, to drive away vice, to teach the rule of faith and to instruct people in sound morals. These men have made a commitment to travel religiously on foot in evangelical poverty, preaching the word of gospel truth.

Now the labourer deserves his food (Matt. 10:10) and it is not right to muzzle the treading ox (1 Cor. 9:9), and the preacher of the gospel ought to live by the gospel (1 Cor. 9:14); accordingly, since these men have come to preach, we desire that they should receive from the diocese their food and all else that is necessary for their support. With the consent of the chapter of the church of St Stephen and of the clergy of the diocese of Toulouse we assign in perpetuity to these preachers, and to any others who are moved by zeal for the Lord and a longing for the salvation of souls to attach themselves to this task of preaching in this manner, one half of the third of the tithes which is devoted to the furnishing and maintenance of the fabric of all the parish churches under our jurisdiction. This is to provide for their clothing and whatever else they may need when they are sick and when they want to rest for a time. We decree that whatever is left over at the end of the year is to revert to the parish churches for their furnishing, or is to be used for the poor, as the bishop sees fit. The law requires that a certain portion of all tithes ought always to be devoted to the poor, and it is evident that we are under a special obligation to devote part of the tithes to those who freely choose evangelical poverty for the sake of Christ and who strive and labour to enrich everyone with the gifts of heaven by their example and teaching. In this way we can appropriately repay those from whom we reap temporal profit, by sowing spiritual seed for them by our own endeavour and by that of others.

Given in the year of the incarnation 1215, in the reign of King Philip of France, Count de Montfort being ruler of Toulouse, I, Fulk, being bishop of Toulouse. [Charter of Bishop Fulk]

ITINERANT PREACHING

When Dominic decided in the year 1206 to devote himself entirely to working for the salvation of his fellow mortals, he resolved at the same time to adopt a specific way of carrying out this purpose, namely the 'apostolic life' or imitation of the apostles. This was one of the things called for by the movement of reform which had been stirring the church since the eleventh century, and it had won many adherents, but in the time of St Dominic it was practised chiefly by heretical preachers. The salient characteristic of this movement is itinerant preaching combined with mendicant poverty. It appeals in this connection to the gospel texts concerning the sending out of Christ's disciples (Matt. 10:5–16; Mark 6:7–13; Luke 9:1–6, 10:1–16) and to the conduct of the apostles on their missionary journeys.

As a canon, Dominic was obliged to be resident in his monastery; nevertheless he adopted the 'apostolic life' and wandered round Languedoc from 1206 to 1215, preaching the truths of the faith and attempting over and over again to enter into conversation with the different groups of heretics. This constant travelling not only exposed him to all sorts of dangers, it also brought home to him that he was only a stranger and a pilgrim on the earth (1 Peter 2:11), without a permanent home. Ultimately it led him to Christ himself.

After the foundation of the order, and especially after the adoption of the Rule of St Augustine, priorities were established, which brought with them a greater degree of stability, but the ideal of itinerant preaching was not abandoned. Friars capable of preaching and educated for it continued to be on the road, always on foot, returning from time to time to the priory to recuperate physically and spiritually. In this way Dominic succeeded in combining stability with the life of wandering, without interfering with the preaching. On the contrary, priories became places where the brethren found community and security, where they assembled for prayer and for initial and continuing education, and precisely in these ways they found new strength for their apostolic undertaking.

During his activity in Languedoc Dominic directed his attention primarily to the debate with heresy, without forgetting the other faithful who found themselves in difficulty there. After the foundation of his order, which was an order of priests, he incorporated the whole spectrum of preaching into his programme: preaching of the truths of the faith, confirming the faith of the people and moral improvement. In this he is distinguished from Catholic itinerant preachers who were predominantly laypeople, who had therefore to confine themselves to exhortations to repentance and the explanation of sound morality. When Dominic obtained from Honorius III the recognition of his order's objective of a preaching apostolate unrestricted by diocesan limits, the regulations of canon law which had been in force until then, reserving the preaching of the faith to the bishops, were shattered and entirely new patterns were created in the realm of the pastoral ministry. Now, alongside the bishops, a religious order had the task of preaching worldwide, and it received its canonical mission to do this directly from the pope. The order had the authority to determine for itself which of its friars should be entrusted with this mission. Furthermore, through the foundation of the first apostolic order in the church, Dominic opened up new paths for organised missionary activity among pagan peoples, without which the Christian Europe of the Middle Ages would be inconceivable.

(132) Brother Ventura said that, when [Dominic] was on the road, he wanted to proclaim the word of God, in person or through others, to almost everyone who joined him on the way.
[Bologna Canonisation Process 3]

(133)   When he was travelling, if he came to a place where the brethren had a priory, he would call the brethren together and give them a sermon, presenting the word of God to them and bringing them great consolation. [Ibid. 4]

(134)   Almost every day, unless he was prevented by something really urgent, he would both preach and give the brethren a conference in the evening, and he wept much and provoked others to tears. [Ibid. 6]

(135)   Brother Rudolph said that [Dominic] was very eager and devoted and assiduous in preaching and in hearing confessions. And he often wept while preaching and stirred his hearers to weep. [Ibid. 33]

(136)   Brother Stephen said that [Dominic] was persistent and zealous in his preaching, and his words were so moving that he often moved himself and his hearers to tears. He said that he had never heard anyone whose words moved the brethren so much to compunction and weeping. He also said that it was his custom always to speak about God or with God, at home or outside or on the road, and he encouraged the brethren to do the same, and even had it put in his constitutions.

[Ibid. 37]

(137)   Brother Frugerio said that [Dominic] always spoke about God, and he used to preach about God to anyone he joined on the road; and he encouraged his friars to do the same, and he had it put in the rule of the Friars Preachers.

[Ibid. 47]

(138)   Abbot William Peire said that St Dominic thirsted passionately for the salvation of souls; he was extremely zealous for souls. He was also so enthusiastic as a preacher that by day and by night, in churches, houses, fields, on the road, everywhere, he wanted to preach the word of the Lord and he encouraged the brethren to do the same and not to talk about anything except God. [Languedoc Canonisation Process 18]

(139)   Brother Buonviso said that, when he was a novice in Bologna and had no experience of preaching, since he had not

yet studied the bible, Brother Dominic told him to go to Piacenza and preach there. He begged to be excused on the
grounds of his inexperience, but Brother Dominic persuaded
him, with the most charming words, that he ought to go. And
he said, 'Go without anxiety, because the Lord will be with
you and will put the word you are to preach in your mouth.'
So he, the witness, obediently went to Piacenza and preached
there and God gave him such grace in his preaching that as a
result of it three brethren entered the Order of Preachers.

[Bologna Canonisation Process 24]

(140)   Brother John of Spain said that [Dominic] was compassionate towards his neighbours and earnestly desired their
salvation. He often used to preach himself and he induced the
brethren in any way that he could to preach and he sent them
out to preach, asking and urging them to be concerned about
the salvation of souls. Because of his great confidence in God
he sent out even simple friars to preach, saying, 'Go without
anxiety, because the Lord will give you the word you are to
preach and he will be with you, and you will lack nothing.' So
out they went, and it all turned out just as he said. [Ibid. 26]

(141)   Truly the holy father was a Jacob in his preaching and
an Israel in his contemplation, so that neither Leah nor Rachel
was lacking to him in this way of life. He used to travel round
and send out his first brethren, even though he had only a
few and they were indifferently educated and mostly young.
Some religious of the Cistercian order were amazed at this and
particularly at the confident way he sent such young friars out
to preach. They set themselves to watch these young men, to
see if they could find some fault with anything they did or said.
He put up with this for some time, but one day, filled with a
holy boldness, he asked them, 'Why do you spy on my disciples,
you disciples of the Pharisees? I know, I know for certain, that
my young men will go out and come back, will be sent out and

will return; but your young men will be kept locked up and still go out.' [Stephen of Salanhac I 7]

(142)   After the death of that renowned prince, Count Simon de Montfort, who died at Toulouse in the Lord's army the day after the Nativity of John the Baptist 1217, when the blessed father Dominic was dispersing the brethren, he sent Peter Seilhan to Limoges, as I have often heard him relate – it was in his hands that I made my profession. He pleaded ignorance and lack of books, having only a few pages of homilies by St Gregory. But St Dominic said to him, 'Go, my son, and go confidently. I will hold you before God twice every day. Do not doubt, you will win many for God and bring forth much fruit.' A short time after that he arrived at Limoges and was received with kindness by the bishop and chapter of Limoges and was given a place to live.[3] Like one of the ancient prophets he was held in great honour in the land among the clergy and people and grew old there in great esteem. He was the first brother of the order after St Dominic. Towards the end of his life he returned to Toulouse, where he had been born, and ended his life in holiness in the Lord on 22 February 1257.

[Ibid. I 8]

(143)   Brother John of Spain said that [Dominic] used to take his shoes off when he was travelling from one place to another and he walked barefoot until he came to the next place and then put his shoes on again. When he left the place he removed them again, and he always carried his shoes himself and did not want anyone else to help carry them. If ever he struck his foot on a stone, he endured it with a cheerful look and was not at all upset. He would say, 'This is a penance', like a man who always rejoiced in his troubles.

[Bologna Canonisation Process 27]

The primitive constitutions of the order prescribe how the brethren should comport themselves when they are sent out to preach:

140

(144)   When those who are suitable for it are to go out to preach, they shall be given a companion by the prior, selected in view of what will, in his judgement, be most beneficial for their manners and good name. After receiving a blessing they are to go out, behaving everywhere like upright, religious men who desire to provide for their own salvation and that of others, like men of the gospel, following in the footsteps of their Saviour, talking either to God or about God, within themselves or with others. They shall avoid being intimate with any dubious companions. When they set off on a journey to practise their task of preaching or when they are going anywhere else, they are neither to accept nor to carry gold, silver, money or gifts of any kind, except for food and necessary clothing and books. Those who are appointed to be preachers or to study are to have no concern or responsibility for temporal affairs, so that they will be free to fulfil their spiritual ministry better, unless there is no one else to provide for the needs of the brethren, because it is sometimes necessary to give time to the particular needs of the day. [Primitive Constitutions II 31]

The choice of preachers

(145)   Those who are considered by some of the brethren to be suitable as preachers are to be presented to the chapter[4] or the diffinitors, as well as those who have been given the task of preaching on the authority of their priors or of some higher superior or chapter. They are all to be examined individually by suitable people appointed by the chapter to deal with this and other questions arising at the chapter, and the brethren with whom they have been living are to be questioned carefully about what grace of preaching they have from God and about their study and religious life and the eagerness of their charity and about their commitment and purpose. After such brethren have given their evidence on these points, they are to make whatever decision seems most useful, on the advice and with the consent of the major superior; that is to say, they must

decide whether these candidates ought to spend time in study or whether they should practise preaching under the supervision of brethren who have had more experience at it or whether they are ready to exercise the office of preacher usefully by themselves. [Ibid. II 20]

Avoiding giving scandal

(146)   Our brethren should be careful not to upset religious or the clergy when they preach by 'setting their mouths against heaven' (Ps. 72:9). If they see anything in them which needs correcting, they should try to put it right by taking them aside and pleading with them as with their fathers (1 Tim. 5:1).

[Ibid. II 33]

On 21 January 1217 Pope Honorius III charged Prior Dominic and the brethren of St Romain in Toulouse to preach the word of God and encouraged them to persevere in this task in spite of every difficulty. With this Bull Honorius confirmed for Dominic and his brethren that preaching was the very reason for their existence. This is the first time that the preaching of the word of God is designated as the objective of a religious order.

(147)   Bishop Honorius, servant of the servants of God, to his beloved sons, the prior and brethren of St Romain, preachers in the district of Toulouse, greetings and our apostolic blessing.
To the giver of all graces we give gracious thanks in the grace of God which is given to you (1 Cor. 1:4), in which you stand (Rom. 5:2) and, as we hope, will stand to the end, because you blaze inwardly with the flame of charity and are fragrant outwardly with the good odour of your reputation, which delights healthy minds and restores those that are sick, to which, as zealous doctors, you apply spiritual medicines, lest they remain unfruitful, fertilising them by your beneficial eloquence with the seed of God's word. Like faithful servants, you expend the talents entrusted to you so that you will be

able to restore them twice over to the Lord. Like unconquered champions of Christ, armed with the shield of faith and the helmet of salvation (Eph. 6:16–17), you do not fear those who can kill the body (Matt. 10:28), but, in the greatness of your heart, you brandish against the enemies of the faith the word of God which is more incisive than any two-edged sword (Heb. 4:12). Thus you hate your life in this world, so that you may keep it for eternal life (Jn 12:25).

However, since it is the outcome, not the fight, that crowns the victor, and only perseverance wins the appointed trophy for those who run the race of all the virtues, we beg your charity and eagerly exhort you, commanding you by our apostolic letter and enjoining it upon you in remission of your sins: more and more be strong in the Lord, striving to preach the good news of God's word, insisting in season and out of season, fulfilling creditably the work of an evangelist (2 Tim. 4:2, 5). And if you endure tribulation because of this, do not merely bear it calmly, but revel in it with the apostle (Rom. 5:3), rejoicing to have been found worthy to suffer insult for the name of Jesus (Acts 5:41). This light moment of tribulation results in an immense weight of glory (2 Cor. 4:17), to which the pains of this present age are not worthy to be compared (Rom. 8:18).

We too, meaning to foster you with our favour as our special sons, ask you to offer the sacrifice of your lips (Hos. 14:3) to the Lord for us, in case we may obtain by your prayers what we are unable to obtain by our own merits.

[Honorius III, Letter of 21 January 1217]

On 12 May 1220 Pope Honorius III commissioned six monks by name, from different monasteries in Italy, to set out to preach with Brother Dominic. Dominic had petitioned the pope to make monks available for his mission in Lombardy. It was not in accordance with tradition that monks should leave their monasteries to preach, but for Dominic the plight of the church took precedence over monastic tradition.[5]

143

(148)   Since those who sow upon the water are blessed (Is. 32:20) and those who hide corn are cursed among the people (Prov. 11:26), you act advisedly if you do not wrap up in a napkin the talent entrusted to you by God (Luke 19:20), since no one lights a lamp and puts it under a bushel; it should be placed on a lampstand to give light to everyone who is in the house (Matt. 5:15).

So, since our beloved son, Brother Dominic, prior of the Order of Preachers, believes that great benefit will accrue to souls if you expend for the good of your neighbours, under his guidance, the grace of preaching you have received from God, we command your good sense, by this apostolic letter, to set out with Brother Dominic for love of him who, out of the great love with which he loved us (Eph. 2:4), went out from the hidden bosom of the Father into the public domain of the human condition. Propound the word of God to those whom Brother Dominic thinks it will benefit, so that those who have gone astray may return to the way of righteousness, once the light of truth has been shown them, knowing that we have given authority to Brother Dominic that you should be obliged to work with him in the service of the word of God, though always wearing your own habits.

[Honorius III, Letter of 12 May 1220]

On 11 March 1221 Pope Honorius III called for all bishops and prelates to support the friars of the Order of Preachers in their activity as preachers among the faithful. This is one of many Bulls of Commendation which Honorius issued for Dominic and his order; it is a document which the friars carried with them as proof that they had their mission to preach from the pope himself.

(149)   Whoever receives a prophet in the name of a prophet will receive the reward of a prophet (Matt. 10:41). We therefore rightly commend to all of you these preachers, who are necessary to holy church, because they minister the food of God's word, so that thereby you may obtain an incomparable reward.

This is why we think it right to commend to you with special urgency our beloved sons, the friars of the Order of Preachers, who, having made profession of poverty and regular life, are entirely deputed to the preaching of the word of God. We ask and earnestly exhort all of you, and we command you by our apostolic letter, when they come to your territory, to welcome them charitably to the office of preacher to which they have been deputed. Eagerly encourage the people who are your subjects to receive the seed of God's word devoutly from their lips and assist them generously in their needs out of respect for God and for us. In addition strive to show them this favour, that by your co-operation they may the more happily run the course of their adopted ministry to its end and win the desired fruit and object of their toil, which is the salvation of souls.

[Honorius III, Letter of 11 March 1221]

The following letter from the bishop of Metz shows how some members of the episcopate understood the significance of the new order and how they promoted the friars.

(150)   Conrad, bishop of Metz by the grace of God, chancellor of the Imperial Court, to all who see these present letters, salvation in the Lord.

As St Gregory bears witness, the highest good which can be possessed in this life is zeal for souls. Led, as we believe and as many good people think, by the inspiration and guidance of the Holy Spirit, the pope has established and confirmed an excellent order, the Order of Friars Preachers. Since it seeks nothing from or in its preaching except only the benefit of souls, we declare to you that we have taken the friars of this order into our favour and good will, devotedly accepting them under our care and protection.

Knowing therefore that, if their order had a house in the city of Metz, their presence among us would not only be of the greatest benefit to the laity because of their preaching, but it would also be extremely useful to the clergy because of their

145

theological lectures, we desire to follow the example of the pope, who gave them a house in Rome, and that of many archbishops and bishops; accordingly we exhort you, for the good of all, to offer advice and help to them in obtaining a place where they can erect a priory inside the city, in accordance with the norms of their order, and we grant to the friars the authority to build a priory in the city of Metz.

Given in Metz, 22 April in the year of the Lord's Incarnation 1221, Frederick II being emperor and Honorius III presiding over the whole church as supreme pontiff, under the lord Gerhard Angebourch as Bürgermeister of Metz.

[Bishop Conrad of Metz, Letter of 22 April 1221]

POVERTY

It was an essential hallmark of the 'apostolic life' to strive after poverty, generally understood as mendicant poverty. This striving after poverty was a religious requirement, based on the words of Jesus and the behaviour of the apostles. Dominic lived this ideal from 1206 until his death. All the same, at the start of the Order of Preachers he made some concessions for his community, although he tried to inspire the first friars with enthusiasm for the practice of mendicancy. The concessions were necessary, on the one hand, because of the order's juridical attachment to the Augustinian branch of religious life, and they were also needed, on the other hand, because of the small number of friars, many of them young, who were mostly still in formation and must therefore not be overtaxed. As soon as the order was strong enough and had secured an incontestable place for itself in the church, Dominic broke away from the Augustinian tradition of religious life, which was unthinkable without real estate and a fixed income. In 1220 he introduced mendicancy, without worrying about the fact that priests were forbidden to beg; not only the individual friars, but the priories too were to live off alms.

This poverty, in Dominic, bears an unmistakably apostolic character. He regarded it always in view of the goal of the order, the preaching of the word of God, and it was subordinated to this goal.

For him poverty did not mean primarily possessing nothing; the friars did, for example, possess their houses and their books, which they required for the performance of their job. Their poverty affected primarily their life and its needs, such as clothing, food and lodging. Through it they gave public witness to that ideal to which they had committed themselves; more than that, in fact, they renounced their position in society and freely chose a place among the little ones, among those whom society despises. They were inspired in this by the thought of following Christ and the apostles. Thus it belonged to their way of life to travel on foot, to spend the night in hostels for the poor, to accept the humiliation of begging, to endure hunger and thirst and, at the same time, to refrain from criticising their fellow men, particularly the religious and clerics of the time.

This attitude was enjoined even by the oldest constitutions of the order. They bid the novice master to teach the novices to practise inner and outer humility, thereby imitating him who said of himself, 'I am meek and humble of heart' (Matt. 11:29). Exterior and interior poverty, understood like this, represented for Dominic at the same time a special kind of penitential life. Even if religious life had always been regarded as a life of penance, preaching the word of God while being constantly on the road in insecurity and in dependence on the material support of other people represented an additional penance, which the letters of Pope Honorius III repeatedly stress. But this inner and outer poverty, linked to a penitential attitude of mind, freed Dominic and his preachers from many cares, so that they could devote themselves entirely to their mission. It gave them great flexibility, as well as making them much less dependent on the great people of the world. Above all it gave them the freedom of charity, from which, in the case of Dominic, flowed a quite particular joy. This joy, which flowed from the inner freedom of love, was reflected in his face and set others alight too.

(151) Brother Amizo said that Master Dominic was a supreme lover of poverty, both with regard to his food and clothing and that of the friars of his order and with regard to the brethren's buildings and churches and their liturgy and the

ornamentation of their ecclesiastical vestments. In his day he was very keen on this and took great pains to see that the brethren did not use purple or silk cloth either for the vestments they wore or on the altars, and that they had no gold or silver vessels except for chalices.

[Bologna Canonisation Process 17]

(152)   Brother John of Spain said that in those days many estates and properties were given to the Order of Preachers in the regions of Toulouse and Albi. He also said that, when the Order of Preachers had all these estates and properties there, and when they used to carry money with them when they were travelling and when they used to ride on horseback and wear surplices, Brother Dominic worked hard to bring it about that the friars of the order would abandon and despise all worldly things and devote themselves to poverty and give up travelling on horseback and live off alms and carry nothing with them when they were on a journey. So the properties they held in the kingdom of France were given to the Cistercian nuns and their other properties were given to other people. And, to enable the brethren to concentrate more on study and preaching, Brother Dominic wanted the order's uneducated laybrothers to have authority over the educated brethren in the administration and provision of temporal goods, but the clerical brethren refused to have the laybrothers given authority over them, in case they should suffer what the brethren of the Order of Grandmont suffered at the hands of their laybrothers. [Ibid. 26]

(153)   He also said that he had a great love of poverty and zealously encouraged the brethren to love it. Asked how he knows this, he replied that Brother Dominic revelled in having cheap clothes, and he abandoned all temporal goods, and he, the witness, was often present when he exhorted the brethren to poverty. [Ibid. 27]

(154)   Brother Rudolph said that Brother Dominic had a great love of poverty and he exhorted the brethren to poverty. He knows this because once, when Brother Dominic came to Bologna, Signor Oderico Galiziani wanted to give the brethren some properties of his worth more than five hundred Bologna pounds. The legal instrument had been drawn up in the presence of the bishop of Bologna, but Brother Dominic had the contract torn up and did not want them to have those or any other properties, he wanted them to live solely by alms, and even that sparingly. If they had enough in the house to live off for one day, he did not want them to accept anything more that day, nor did he send anyone out for alms. He wanted them to have small houses and cheap clothes. Even in church he did not want them to use silk; their vestments were to be of buckram or some other cloth. He did not want the brethren to interfere in temporal affairs or in the business of the house or in discussions of its material concerns, except for those who were responsible for looking after the house; all the others he wanted to be always intent on reading, prayer and preaching. And if he knew any friar to be useful for preaching, he did not want any other job given him. [Ibid. 32]

(155)   Brother Stephen said that he had first met Master Dominic, the founder and originator of the Order of Friars Preachers and its first master, fifteen years and more ago, and, even before he knew him personally by sight, he heard much good spoken of him by important people whose word was reliable. He had heard that, when he was prior or subprior of the church of Osma, where he was a canon, he studied theology at Palencia. And while he was there a dreadful famine began to prevail in that part of the world, so that many poor people were dying there of starvation. So Brother Dominic, moved by compassion and pity, sold his books, which were annotated in his own hand, and gave their price and the other things which he possessed to the poor, saying, 'I refuse to study on dead skins, while people are dying of hunger.' His example was

followed by some people of great authority, and from that time onwards they began to preach with him. [Ibid. 35]

(156) He often heard Brother Dominic preaching and exhorting the brethren to poverty. If ever he or the community was offered any properties, he refused to accept them, nor would he allow the brethren to accept them. He wanted them to have cheap, small houses. He himself wore the cheapest habit and cheap clothes. Asked how he knows this, he replied that he frequently saw him wearing a very cheap habit and a short scapular, nor was he willing to cover it with his cappa, even in the presence of important people. He also said that at St Nicholas's the brethren had very mean, small cells, so Brother Rudolph, who was the procurator, began to raise some of the cells, in the absence of Brother Dominic, to make them a foot or so higher. When Brother Dominic returned and saw the cells that had been raised, he began to weep and repeatedly rebuked Brother Rudolph and the other brethren, saying to him and the others, 'Do you so quickly want to abandon poverty and build great palaces?' So he ordered them to leave off the work, which thus remained unfinished as long as he was alive. As he had loved poverty in himself, he loved it in his brethren too, so he ordered them to use cheap clothes and never to carry money when they were on the road, but everywhere to live off alms, and he had this written into his rule.

[Ibid. 38]

(157) Brother Paul of Venice said that [Dominic] wore the cheapest possible habit, and when he left the road at his departure from any town he would take his shoes off and walk barefoot. He often saw this when he was travelling with him. He sometimes saw Brother Dominic going from door to door begging alms and accepting bread like a pauper. At Dugliolo once, when he was begging alms, someone gave him a whole loaf of bread and the father knelt down to receive it with great

humility and devotion. He wanted the friars to live off alms and he, the witness, often heard him saying so to them.

[Ibid. 42]

(158)   Brother Frugerio said that [Dominic] used one tunic in winter and summer alike. He loved poverty and exhorted his brethren to do so too. Asked how he knows this, he replied that he saw him wearing a cheap habit and heard him exhorting his brethren to embrace poverty and to love it. If he discovered any of the friars wearing clothes that deserved rebuke because of their price or form, he would correct and punish him at once. He loved poverty to such an extent that he did not want the brethren to accept properties, but to live off alms. And he had this written into the rule of the friars. He wanted them to have cheap houses and cheap reading-desks, so that in everything they would give an impression of cheapness and poverty.

[Ibid. 47]

(159)   The priest, Pierre Brunet, said that once, when [Dominic] had crossed some water in a ferry, the sailors demanded a denier from him for their fare. He had no way of paying, so they insistently demanded either payment or some security and to this end they would not let him go. He fixed his eyes on the ground and showed them a denier saying, 'Take from the ground what you want from me.' They took the denier and let him go. [Languedoc Canonisation Process 14]

(160)   It occurs to me incidentally to mention something about Brother John of Navarre, which I heard him relate himself. When the holy father Dominic was sending him to Paris with Brother Laurence, John asked to be given some provisions or some money for the journey. The saint refused to give him any, urging them to go like disciples of Christ, not carrying gold or silver. 'Trust in the Lord,' he said, 'for those who fear God lack nothing.' John would not accept this, but absolutely refused to obey the saint's word. When the holy and loving father saw

the wretched man's disobedience, he fell at his feet, weeping and howling for the miserable man who would not weep for himself. He told them to give him just twelve deniers for the journey all the way to Paris. [Stephen of Salanhac III 7:8]

(161) In 1220 the first general chapter of the order was held in Bologna. This chapter decreed that our brethren should thereafter no longer hold properties or revenues and that they should give up those they already held in the district round Toulouse. [Jordan, *Libellus* 86–87]

(162) In no way are properties or revenues to be accepted. None of our friars is to dare to take steps or make petitions with a view to obtaining benefices for his relations.

[Primitive Constitutions II 26]

(163) Our friars are to have modest houses, which are not too big. The walls are not to exceed a height of fifteen feet without an attic, or twenty-five feet with an attic, and the church is not to exceed thirty-eight feet. And it is not to have a stone vault except perhaps over the choir and the sacristy.[6]

[Ibid. II 35]

STUDY

What most distinguishes Dominic from the traditional orders in the church is the new element which he introduced into religious life and to which he devoted a considerable part of his legislation: study. It replaced the manual labour of the monks, which even groups of canons and various circles that included the 'apostolic life' in their programme had adopted. Among the Catharists and the Waldensians, the Poor Catholics and the Poor Lombards, by contrast, the study of scripture was an important priority, but all the same they orientated it too much to their own intellectual benefit or the struggle against deviant tendencies. With Dominic study, like poverty, serves the preaching of the gospel. He did not confine himself to those truths of the faith on which he had to fall back in debating with heretical movements, but he endeavoured to penetrate intellectually the entire content of the faith.

Thereby Dominic responded to one of the greatest weaknesses of the church of that time, the theological ignorance of a great part of the clergy and the inadequate evangelisation of the people which resulted from it. Because study was intimately linked to the goal of the order and constituted an essential prerequisite for credible preaching, Dominic shifted several of the traditions of religious life to make sure that they would not impede study. By dispensing them from various obligations he secured for talented students the possibility of devoting themselves to study without being interrupted. The friars who were destined to be preachers had to spend several years in the study of theology, and when they returned from their work outside the priory they were to use their time in continuing their education. In every priory there was a teacher of theology (a lector) responsible for the initial and further education of the friars. Apart from making possible a more solid style of preaching, study also served the personal intellectual enrichment of the brethren, in which they found fresh nourishment for their prayer.

Thanks to the introduction of study into the constitutions of his order. Dominic was not only a trailblazer for his own time, he had a decisive influence on entire generations. In theological faculties, where the Dominicans soon acquired their first chairs, theological science entered upon a period of great prosperity, the intellectual and spiritual formation of the clergy was generally improved, and new avenues to the sources of mysticism were opened up. So, beside study, religious experience too received new ground in which to flourish.

(164) Afterwards Dominic was sent to Palencia to be formed in the liberal arts, because there was a thriving arts faculty there at this time. When he thought he had learned enough of the arts, he abandoned them and fled to the study of theology, as if he was afraid to waste his limited time on less fruitful study. He began to develop a passionate appetite for God's

words, finding them 'sweeter than honey to his mouth' (Ps. 118:103). [Jordan, *Libellus* 6]

In his controversies with the heretics in the south of France, he recognised the urgent need for solid theological training. He took his first friars to Toulouse to study with an English professor of theology, Alexander Stavensby, who was teaching there.

(165)   A certain master was teaching in Toulouse, who was outstanding in his birth, his knowledge and his reputation. One morning before daybreak he was looking over his lectures when he was overcome by weariness and leaned his head for a while on his chair and went to sleep. At that very time he seemed to see seven stars being presented to him. While he was wondering greatly at the strangeness of such a gift, they suddenly increased in brilliance and in size until their light filled the whole country, the whole world. Immediately he woke up and saw that it was daybreak, so he called his servants to carry his books and went to his lecture room, and there St Dominic with six companions wearing the same habit came to him humbly, informing him that they were brethren who were preaching the gospel of God in the territory of Toulouse for the faithful and against unbelievers, and they indicated that they had come to attend his class and that they would very much like to listen to his lectures. Over a long period this master enjoyed the devoted intimacy of the seven brethren and he taught them as his students. Recalling the vision he had seen shortly before, he understood that the brilliant stars were St Dominic and his companions, and he saw them suddenly blaze up in an immense light of fame and knowledge. As a result he treated them with the greatest respect and always from that time onwards took them to his heart with the warmest affection. He told this story to Brother Arnulf of Béthune and his companion, when they were in England at the king's court. [Humbert 40]

Dominic went so far as to ask Honorius III to get some of the professors and students in the university of Paris to go to Toulouse, so that they could teach the Friars Preachers there and help them in their difficult task. Had Dominic not soon changed his mind, he would probably have brought about indirectly the foundation of the university of Toulouse. On 19 January 1217 Honorious III requests of the professors and students of theology in Paris that some of their number should proceed to the territory of Toulouse to assist there in the work of converting the heretics.

(166)   If that land which has, as it were, just been ploughed up for the first time is not cultivated by new farmers and settlers, the weeds which have been rooted out will spring up again and poisonous snakes will seek refuge there and so the last state will be worse than the first (Luke 11:26). Therefore noticing that, by God's grace, there are many among you whose delight is in the law of the Lord and who have long been sitting by the harvest of teaching[7] like trees planted beside streams of water (Ps. 1:2–3), so that they could henceforth bear fruit better if they were transplanted, we earnestly beg and exhort all of you, commanding you by our apostolic letter, that some of you would go [to Toulouse] to work there wholeheartedly for the cause of God, applying yourselves vigilantly to lecturing, preaching and exhortation, administering the grace of God to one another as good dispensers of his manifold grace (1 Pet. 4:10), so that the old Jebusite may be banished and the people made acceptable to God. [Honorius III, Letter of 19 January 1217]

Despite his emphasis on poverty, Dominic did not forgo the possession of books, which were at that time quite a luxury. He impressed upon his brethren a love for books and an enthusiasm for study. He resolved to send some of his first friars to the most famous university of the epoch, the university of Paris.

(167)   A party of friars was also sent to Paris: Brother Matthew, who had been elected abbot, with Brother Bertrand,

who was later provincial of Provence, a man of great holiness and ruthless self-discipline, in that he mortified his flesh savagely and had taken to heart in many ways the model and example of Master Dominic, whose travelling companion he had sometimes been. These two were sent to Paris with letters from the pope, to make the order known there. With them went two brethren who were to study there, Brother John of Navarre and Brother Laurence the Englishman. Before they reached Paris a great deal of what was to happen to the friars there was revealed by the Lord to Brother Laurence, about the houses they would live in and where they were going to be and about the number of novices they were going to receive. He told them about all this, and events proved him right. A second, separate party was also sent to Paris, consisting of Brother Mamés,[8] Master Dominic's half brother, and Brother Miguel of Spain. They took with them a Norman laybrother called Oderic. [Jordan, *Libellus* 51]

(168)   Brother John of Spain said that Brother Dominic often encouraged and exhorted the friars of the order by word and by his letters to be always studying the New Testament and the Old. He knows this because he heard him talking like this and saw his letters. He also said that he always carried with him the gospel of Matthew and the letters of Paul and he studied them a lot, so that he almost knew them by heart.

[Bologna Canonisation Process 29]

The oldest constitutions of the order contain several prescriptions about study, which reveal its importance for the order as an essential means to its goal. It was the first order in the history of the church to give itself a detailed law about study.

(169)   The superior is to have the right to dispense the brethren in his own community whenever it seems useful to him, particularly in things which seem likely to obstruct study or preaching or the good of souls, since our order is known to

have been founded initially precisely for the sake of preaching and the salvation of souls, and all our concern should be primarily and passionately directed to this all-important goal, that we should be able to be useful to the souls of our neighbours.

[Primitive Constitutions, Prologue]

(170)   The novice master should teach the novices how careful they must be with books and clothes and other things belonging to the monastery. He should teach them how intent they should be in study, always reading something or going over what they have read in their minds, by day and by night, in the house and when they are on a journey, and striving to retain as much as they can in their memories. He should teach them how enthusiastic they ought to be in preaching at suitable times.

[Ibid. I 13]

(171)   A new community should not be launched if it falls short of twelve friars, nor without permission from the general chapter, nor without a prior and a teacher. [Ibid. II 23]

(172)   Careful attention must be paid to students, so they are to have some particular friar without whose permission they are not to copy books or attend lectures. If he sees that they need correcting in any way related to study, he should correct them, and if the matter is beyond his power, he should explain the situation to the superior. They are not to study the books of the pagans and the philosophers, except for a brief inspection of them. They are not to learn secular sciences nor even the so-called liberal arts, but they are to read only books of theology; this applies to the young and to everyone else. [Ibid. II 28]

(173)   Those who are studying are to be dispensed by the superior in such a way as to ensure that they are not lightly drawn away from their study or hindered in it by the Office or anything else. As the master of students sees fit, a special place

is to be set aside where they can meet, in his presence, to raise difficulties and questions after the disputation or after vespers or at any other time when they are free. When one of them is raising a question or expounding something, the others are to keep silent to avoid interrupting him. And if anyone offends by raising questions or taking part in a disputation in any capacity in an impolite or unruly or noisy or obstinate way, he should be rebuked immediately by the person who is in charge of them at the time. Not all the students are to be assigned cells, but only those who are likely to benefit from them in the judgement of their master. And if anyone is found not to be fruitful in study, his cell is to be given to someone else and he is to be put to work in other tasks. They can read and write and pray and sleep in their cells and, if they want to, they can also keep a light burning at night and stay up to study.

[Ibid. II 29]

ᘓ 8 ᘔ

DOMINIC AND WOMEN

It was entirely in line with the 'apostolic life' that both Catholic and heretical itinerant preachers in the twelfth and early thirteenth centuries had women with them, a feature which seems to have spread gradually. Exceptionally we also hear of women preaching in the 'schools' or hospices of the heretics. These institutions resembled more monastic institutions, providing education for young girls and offering hospitality to itinerant preachers. Catholic preachers who settled down and founded monasteries reserved part of their establishments for women and continued to care for them; this is how so-called 'double monasteries' came into existence. But travelling around with women, especially at the beginning of the thirteenth century, fell into disrepute. During his preaching in Languedoc with Bishop Diego and the papal legates Dominic from the outset won over some women to follow Christ, certainly including some converts from heresy. For them he founded the monastery of Prouille, which subsequently became an important element in the 'Holy Preaching' and, later, in the Order of Preachers. In the first period of its existence it performed much the same functions as the hospices of the Albigensians: material support for the itinerant preachers and, probably, accommodation for women and girls who were threatened by heresy. The spiritual care of women was, for Dominic, an essential part of his apostolic programme and it sprang from his natural disposition. In this he was following the example of Christ and the apostles (Luke 8:1–3; 23:49, 55; 24:10, 22; Rom. 16:1–15; 1 Cor. 9:5). In addition, the major religious orders were at this time trying to hold in check the great throng of women eager to push their way into religious life, a movement which was then at its peak; they wanted to exclude monasteries of women from their associations and to give up responsibility for them. This meant that women were being pushed to the edge even in the church. In society they were already marginalised, apart from the small class of noble ladies, who were idolised in chivalrous and courtly convention and celebrated by the minnesingers. This stratum of society Dominic encountered but rarely. He was dealing chiefly with poor, suffering, exploited, misled and degraded women, to whom almost no one paid any attention, despite their desire for religious life. He accordingly incorporated the spiritual care of women consciously in his plans. In addition to the monastery of Prouille he started a monastery for women in Madrid and obliged the friars there to put their house at the disposal of the sisters. In Bologna he wanted to forgo the enlargement of the brethren's priory in favour of building a house for the sisters. But his most significant undertaking in this domain was the reform of the Roman nuns and the foundation of the reformed monastery at San Sisto, which had a decisive influence on the later development of religious life for women; thanks to the life of the sisters and the rule which Dominic gave them, San Sisto provided a model which others were soon to follow.

(174)   In Bologna Master Dominic was now approaching the end of his earthly pilgrimage and began to be seriously ill. He called twelve of the more sensible brethren to his sick-bed and exhorted them to be eager in their practice of the religious life.[1] 'Look at me,' he said, 'God's mercy has preserved me to this day in bodily virginity, but I confess that I have not escaped from the imperfection of being more excited by the conversation of young women than by being talked to by old women.'

[Jordan, *Libellus* 92]

Right at the start of his preaching in southern France beside Bishop Diego and the papal legates Dominic addressed himself to women too, as we learn from a letter of Archbishop Bérenger of Narbonne (17 April 1207). He was presenting the newly founded monastery for women at Prouille with the church of St Martin, Limoux: 'We freely grant to the prioress and nuns who have recently been converted by the counsel and example of Brother Dominic of Osma and his companions the church of St Martin, Limoux.'

Jordan ascribed the foundation of the monastery solely to Bishop Diego. After Bishop Diego's departure, though, responsibility for the monastery fell to Dominic. After the establishment of the new order, it was incorporated into it.

(175)   At a place called Prouille, between Fanjeaux and Montréal, Bishop Diego established a monastery to receive certain noble women whose parents had been forced by poverty to entrust them to the heretics to be educated and brought up. To this day the handmaids of Christ there offer acceptable service to their Maker, leading vigorously holy lives in outstanding innocence and purity. A life such as theirs is conducive to salvation for those who lead it, an example to others, a joy to the angels and pleasing to God. [Ibid. 27]

Remarkable stories were told in the neighbourhood about the conversion of some of these women, such as this one, which was reported during Dominic's Canonisation Process by a woman who claimed to have been an eye-witness, and which was later written up for inclusion in the life of Dominic used in the Office:

(176)   On one occasion the man of God, Dominic, preached in a town called Fanjeaux, proving the Catholic faith and refuting in many ways the bad faith of the heretics. Afterwards, as he usually did, he remained in the church to pray. Nine noble ladies from the town came into the church and threw themselves at his feet saying, 'Servant of God, help us. If what you have been preaching today is true, then our minds have for a long time been blinded by a spirit of error. To this day we have believed in the people you call heretics, whom we call "good men", and we have adhered to them wholeheartedly. Now we cannot make up our minds. Servant of God, help us; pray to the Lord your God to make known to us the faith that is his, in which we can live and die and find salvation.'

[Constantine 48]

(177)   The man of God stood still for a little while, praying silently. Then he said to them, 'Be firm and wait without fear. I trust in the Lord my God that he, who desires no one to be lost (2 Pet. 3:9), will show you now what sort of lord you have been attached to so far.' At once they saw the most revolting cat jump out from among them, as big as a large dog, with great blazing eyes and a long, wide, bloody tongue reaching all the way to its navel; it had a short tail, which was sticking up, so that it showed its disgusting rump wherever it turned, emitting an unbearable stench. It pranced around these ladies for a certain time and then, climbing up the rope from which the bell was suspended, it finally disappeared through the bell tower, leaving foul traces behind it. Turning to the ladies, the man of God encouraged them saying, 'You can see what sort of being you have been serving in following the heretics from that image that our own eyes have witnessed by God's act.' They gave thanks to God and from that time onwards they were completely converted to the Catholic faith and some of them even took the religious habit with the sisters of Prouille.

[Ibid. 49]

In 1215 Bishop Fulk donated a hospice in Toulouse to Dominic, who tried to establish another monastery for women there; but the funds were insufficient, so he was obliged to abandon his plan. He was more successful in Madrid in 1219. The only personal letter to survive from Dominic's hand is one addressed to the nuns of Madrid.

(178)   Brother Dominic, Master of the Preachers, to the dear prioress of Madrid and all the nuns in the community, greetings. May you make progress every day!

I am delighted at the fervour with which you follow your holy way of life, and thank God for it. He has indeed freed you from the squalor of this world. Fight the good fight, my daughters, against our ancient foe, fight him insistently with fasting and prayers, because no one will win the crown of victory without engaging in the context in the proper way (2 Tim. 2:5).

Until now you have had no place in which you could practise your religious life, but now you can no longer offer that excuse. By the grace of God you have buildings that are quite suitable enough for religious observance to be maintained. From now on I want you to keep the silence in the prescribed places, namely the refectory, the dormitory and the oratory, and to observe your rule fully in everything else too. Let none of the sisters go outside the gate, and let nobody come in, except for the bishop or any other ecclesiastical superior, who comes to preach to you or on visitation. Do not be shy of using the discipline or keeping vigil. Be obedient to your prioress. Do not chatter with each other or waste your time gossiping.

Because we can offer you no help in temporal affairs, we do not want to burden you by allowing any of the brethren any authority to receive women or make them members of your community; only the prioress, on the advice of the community, is to have such authority.

Furthermore, I instruct my dear brother [Mamés], who has worked so hard to bring you to this holy state of life, to organise you and make whatever arrangements he considers useful to enable you to conduct yourselves in the most religious and holy way. I also give him power to visitate you and correct you and, if necessary, to remove the prioress from office, provided that a majority of the nuns agree. I also authorise him to grant you any dispensations he thinks appropriate.

Farewell in Christ. [Letter of St Dominic]

During his various stays in Rome he directed his care to the poorest among women, the so-called recluses, that is, women who were voluntarily imprisoned for Christ, who were immured beside a church or in the city walls, living in great wretchedness.

(179) We are invited to visit people in captivity by the example of the saints, including saints living here on earth, of

163

whom the apostle says, 'You had compassion on those in chains' (Heb. 10:34). About St Dominic I was told by Bartholomew de la Cluse, archdeacon of Mâcon and canon of Chartres, that when he was in Rome, after attending his Office, St Dominic went round the walls of the city almost every day, and other places where there were recluses, giving them advice for their salvation, like Tobias who 'visited all who were in captivity and gave them advice for their salvation' (Tob. 1:15)

[Stephen of Bourbon 158]

Sister Cecilia gives us an account of two recluses in Rome, for whom Dominic provided. Here is what she says about one of them:

(180)   There was a recluse living behind the church of St Anastasia, called Sister Lucy, whom Sister Cecilia too had seen several times before she was in the monastery. She had a very serious disease in one arm, which had progressively eaten away all the skin and flesh until the bare bone was visible all the way up to the elbow. Since St Dominic was frequently passing by there on his way to San Sisto, he often used to visit her. So one day, when he visited her with Brother Bertrand the Spaniard and several others, he made her show him the arm in which she had the disease. When she had shown it to him, he made the sign of the cross over it, then he gave her a blessing and went away. But she recovered her health perfectly by the merits of St Dominic. [Cecilia 13]

(181)   A certain lady of the family of the Buvalischi, a widow, a citizen of Rome from the parish of St Saviour in Pisile, whose name was Tutadonna, had great devotion to St Dominic. She had an only son and the young boy was seriously ill. So one day, when St Dominic was preaching in Rome at the church of St Mark, this lady passionately wanted to hear the word of God from his lips, so she left her son, ill as he was, and went to the church where St Dominic was preaching the word of God. At

the end of the sermon she went home and found her son dead. She was overwhelmed by terrible grief, but she hid her grief in silence, trusting in the power of God and the merits of St Dominic. Taking her maids with her, she went to St Dominic at the church of San Sisto, where he was living at the time with the brethren, bringing her dead son with her. Because the house at San Sisto was being prepared to receive the sisters, other people also often went in, taking the opportunity provided by the builders. So she went in and found him standing by the door of the chapter room, as if he was waiting for something there. When she saw him, she put her son at his feet and prostrated herself before him and began to beg him with tears to restore her son to her alive and well. Then St Dominic, moved by her terrible grief, withdrew for a while and said a short prayer. After his prayer he got up and went to the boy and made the sign of the cross over him, then, taking his hand, he raised him up living and restored him safe and sound to his mother, bidding her tell no one about it. But she went home very happily with her son and revealed what had happened to her and her son, so that it reached the ears of the pope, and he wanted to inform everybody about it in a public sermon. But St Dominic, being a true lover and keeper of humility, would not allow him to do this, telling him that if he did it, he would go overseas to the Saracens and would not stay in this part of the world any longer. Afraid that he really would do this, the pope refrained from publicising the miracle.

[Ibid. 1]

Dominic took on the Roman nuns and tried to carry into effect Innocent III's plan to reform them and to establish a reformed monastery for them. He succeeded in reforming one monastery, which had abandoned all discipline, and in bringing the sisters into the new monastery at San Sisto. This became a model monastery, with the rule which Dominic gave it. It served as an example for the reform elsewhere of sisters' convents. Thanks to archival documents we are well informed about this reform. Cecilia also gives us some valuable details.

(182) Pope Honorius, of happy memory, commissioned St Dominic to unite all the nuns who were living in different monasteries in different parts of Rome and to make them live at San Sisto. St Dominic asked him if he would be so kind as to let him have some suitable assistants to help him accomplish such a large task. The pope gave him as his assistants the Lord Ugolino, Bishop of Ostia, who was later pope, and the Lord Stephen of Fossanova, Cardinal of the Holy Apostles, and the Lord Nicholas, Cardinal Bishop of Tusculum, to support him in anything he needed. However all the nuns opposed the scheme and refused, as far as they could, to obey the pope and St Dominic. Only the abbess of Santa Maria in Tempulo, together with all her nuns except one, put herself in Dominic's hands with all the properties and revenues which belonged to the monastery. With the three cardinals who had been given him as his assistants, St Dominic arranged for them all to assemble at San Sisto on Ash Wednesday, after the imposition of ashes, so that the abbess could resign her office in their presence and in the presence of all the nuns and hand over to him and his assistants all the rights of the monastery. [Ibid. 2]

(183) When St Dominic was assembling the nuns who lived in the various monasteries in Rome to unite them, in accordance with the command of Pope Honorius, at the church of San Sisto, where the friars were then living, among others the abbess of Santa Maria in Tempulo made profession in the hands of St Dominic, together with Sister Cecilia and all the nuns except one. The image of the Blessed Virgin, which is now in the church of San Sisto, was then in the monastery of Santa Maria in Tempulo and the abbess promised that she and her nuns would enter San Sisto on condition that this image of Our Lady stayed with them there; but if it returned to its own church, as it had done before, then she and all the other nuns

would not be bound by the profession they had made to St Dominic. He willingly accepted this condition. When they had made their profession, St Dominic told them that he did not want them to go outside the monastery any more to visit their relations or to go anywhere else. When they heard what had happened, the nuns' relations came to the monastery and began to attack the abbess and the nuns for wanting to ruin such a noble monastery and for being willing to place themselves of their own accord in the hands of a rascal of whom no one had ever heard before. As a result, some of the nuns regretted the profession they had made. St Dominic was aware in spirit of what was going on, so one morning he came to them and, after he had said Mass for them and given them a sermon, he said, 'My daughters, you have already changed your minds and wish to withdraw your feet from the way of the Lord. So I want all of you who desire to enter of your own free will to make profession again in my hands.' Then the abbess, with the others, made profession again in his hands. Even though some of them had regretted their previous profession, they were called back to fidelity by his merits.

When they had made their profession again, with the same condition as before, St Dominic took all the keys and thereafter had full authority over the monastery. He appointed some laybrothers to guard the monastery by day and by night, and they provided the sisters (who were now enclosed) with their food and all they needed. And he did not let them any longer speak privately with their relations or with anybody else.

When the pope had given the friars the church of Santa Sabina and they had moved there to live, taking all their utensils and books and everything else, St Dominic wanted the abbess and the other sisters to come and live in San Sisto. So on the first Sunday of Lent they went in to live there. And first of them all Sister Cecilia, who was at that time some seventeen years old, received the habit from St Dominic as she entered the doorway and made profession in his hands for the third time, followed by the abbess and all the nuns of her monastery and by so many other religious and seculars that all together there were forty-four of them.

The following night, after the nuns had entered, St Dominic, with two cardinals – Cardinal Nicholas and Cardinal Stephen, whose nephew St Dominic had restored to life – and many other people, brought the image of the Blessed Virgin on his shoulders to the church of San Sisto. He did this at night for fear of the Romans, who did not want the image to be moved from where it was, because they could see it more easily there. They brought it to San Sisto with many lights going before and after it, and they all walked barefooted, while the sisters waited barefooted in prayer, and the image was placed with great reverence in the sisters' church, and it is there to this day, with the sisters, to the praise of our Lord Jesus Christ, to whom be honour and glory for ever and ever. Amen. [Ibid. 14]

In Bologna too Dominic endeavoured to establish a monastery for women. The central figure in the story is Diana, the intelligent and attractive daughter of the D'Andalò family.

(184) In the course of the year 1218 some Friars Preachers were sent to Bologna from Rome by St Dominic. When they arrived there, they asked for the church of St Nicholas from Brother Rudolph, who was the priest of that church. The church was situated in a place called 'The Vines', which belonged to Signor Andalò, the father of that most illustrious woman, Donna Diana. This Signor Andalò was unwilling to give the place to the friars, but at the pleading of Donna Diana, who later founded the house of St Agnes, he gave his consent and granted them the place. The friars built a house there and a cloister and, by the grace of Christ, they began to increase in numbers.

Meanwhile Master Reginald came to Bologna and began to preach the word of God with great zeal, and Donna Diana, the daughter of Signor Andalò, the gentleman we have mentioned, drawn by the Spirit of God, began to spurn the glamour and

vanities of the world and to spend more time in the company
of the Friars Preachers and in conversation with them. So when
St Dominic came to Bologna she began to love him with all
the affection of her heart and to discuss with him the salvation
of her soul. Not very long afterwards she put herself in his
hands and made profession in the presence of Master Reginald
and some other brethren, namely Brother Guala of Brescia and
Brother Rudolph, and some ladies who are still alive today.
This took place at the altar of St Nicholas. Many other noble
ladies and illustrious women of Bologna followed her example
and began to spend time with the Friars Preachers, conversing
with them about the salvation of their souls. As a result great
devotion was aroused among many noble gentlemen and rela-
tives of these ladies, and they began to help and respect the
friars.

Meanwhile Donna Diana did not forget her vow; she began
to discuss with St Dominic how she could put it into effect. So
one day St Dominic gathered his brethren and asked them
what they thought about building a house of nuns which would
be called, and which would be, a part of the order. The brethren
answered as they thought fit, and then St Dominic said to them,
'I do not want to reply today, I want to consult the Lord. I will
give you my answer tomorrow.' And, as was his custom, he
applied himself to prayer. The next day, after he had prayed,
he sat down with the brethren in chapter and said, 'It is absolutely necessary, brethren, that a house of nuns should be built,
even if it means interrupting the work on our own house.'

When he was about to leave Bologna, St Dominic entrusted
the business to four of the brethren, Master Paul of Hungary,
Brother Guala, who was later bishop of Brescia, Brother
Ventura of Verona, who later became provincial, and Brother
Rudolph of Faenza, of whom mention has already been made.
So, during the lifetime of St Dominic, these four brethren
found a site where the house of nuns was to be built; but the
bishop of Bologna refused permission for a church to be built
there, because it was too close to the city.

Meanwhile Donna Diana was living in her father's house, in the flesh, that is, not in her mind. She wore a hair shirt next to the skin and and an iron chain round her waist, but above them she wore purple and silk and jewels, and gold and silver. She stayed in her room in prayer and silence from early morning until the time of terce.

Since fear of her family prevented her from fulfilling her desire and her promise to St Dominic, to build a house of nuns which would belong to the Order of Preachers and be so called, one day, on the feast of St Mary Magdalene, she announced that she wanted to visit the monastery called Ronzano. So she went to the house there in grand and glorious style, with a great throng of ladies attending her. But when she reached the place, she went alone into the sisters' dormitory and suddenly asked for the habit, and was given it.

As soon as the ladies who had come with her realised what she had done, they sent a messenger to the city. At once a huge crowd formed of men and women, friends and relations. They came to the monastery and dragged her out with such violence that they broke one of her ribs, and she carried the mark of the fracture until the day she died. Because of the injury which they did her that day she lay sick for about a year in her father's house.

The blessed father Dominic was in Bologna at the time and when he heard of her entry he was immensely pleased, but afterwards, when he heard of the injuries she had sustained, he was very sorry for her. While she was lying sick in her father's house he sent letters to her in secret, because her parents would not allow her to speak with anybody unless one of the family was present.

During this period St Dominic passed happily on to eternal joys. Sister Diana remained like this in her father's house, and she was very distressed at the death of such a father as Dominic. But almighty God, who had chosen her before the foundation of the world (Eph. 1:4), did not abandon her. Bit by bit he mercifully removed the obstacles from her path, and she began to recover from her great infirmity. When she was a little better, she fled one night, on the feast of All Saints; she left her father's house and went back to the same monastery as before. Her parents then despaired of her and left her there. So she stayed in that monastery from All Saints up to the week after the Ascension.[2]

During this period Master Jordan, of blessed memory, who was at that time provincial of Lombardy, came faithfully to her assistance, together with the other brethren to whom St Dominic had entrusted the business. They began to take steps to bring the project to the fulfilment which had been for so long desired. As we have said, the bishop would not allow a church to be built in the place mentioned above, because it was too near the city; so the brethren, supported by Diana's family, asked for another place, Valsampietro, as it was called then; later it was called Mount St Agnes. They obtained the bishop's permission and began to build a tiny little house there. When it was built, Master Jordan and other friars of the same order, Brother Guala, Brother Ventura of Verona, Brother Rudolph of Faenza, Brother Bernard the German and some others, went to fetch her and installed her in the little house with four other ladies from Bologna in the year 1223, in the octave of the Ascension. On the feast of the apostles Peter and Paul they received the habit of the order from Master Jordan.

[Chronicle of St Agnes, Bologna]

NOTES

All notes are by Simon Tugwell

1 THE FIGURE OF DOMINIC IN ITS HISTORICAL CONTEXT

1 In fact Innocent had been requesting armed intervention from the outset, and explicitly called for a crusade in November 1207, before the assassination of his legate. The assassination prompted him to renew this call with greater urgency. Cf. *AFP* 65 (1995), p. 40.

2 Probably they actually used the phrase 'order of preaching'; cf. *AFP* 65 (1995), pp. 23–28.

3 According to another, possibly more reliable account, this vision occurred in 1215, during the visit of Dominic and Fulk to Innocent III. Cf. *AFP* 65 (1995), pp. 31–32.

4 There is actually no evidence that Dominic was in any way involved with the San Sisto project before November 1219, though he certainly had some contact with at least one of the Roman monasteries, Santa Maria in Tempulo, before he went to Spain in 1218. Cf. *AFP* 65 (1995), pp. 99–119.

5 The extent and, in particular, the anti-heretical nature of Dominic's preaching in northern Italy in 1220–1221 have been much exaggerated by twentieth-century historians. It is known only that Dominic undertook two journeys in Lombardy and one to the Veneto in this time, and all the evidence suggests that he simply preached wherever he went; nothing indicates that he was engaged in a mission against heretics. Cf. *AFP* 66 (1996), pp. 33–46.

6 Or perhaps not until January 1221. Cf. *AFP* 66 (1996), pp. 55–59, 118.

7 It remained there until the nuns moved to Magnanapoli, where the Angelicum now stands, in 1575; in 1931 the monastery, complete with the icon, was transferred to Monte Mario.

8 The assertion that the order was divided into provinces in 1221 has long been traditional, but it rests solely on the authority of Bernard Gui, who himself quickly repudiated it. I intend to take up the question of how and when provinces evolved in an article in *AFP* in 1997. What is certain is that the 1221 chapter launched an impressive expansion of the order into new territories.

3 DOMINIC'S APOSTOLIC LIFE

1 There has been great debate about the significance of Innocent's advice to Dominic. Building on Fr Koudelka's interpretation and on some previously overlooked evidence, I have argued that it was Innocent who proposed that the Toulouse preaching order should be transformed into a worldwide order and that, to this end, it should adopt an established and uncontroversial Rule. Cf. *AFP* 65 (1995), pp. 6–35.

5 THE PERSONALITY OF DOMINIC

1 It is inconceivable that Dominic had a hairshirt made of panther-hair; the Latin word *pardus* here probably veils an Occitan original either referring to the colour of the hair or to the local grey bear.

6 SPEAKING WITH GOD

1 'To speak with God or about God' is the text found in the Constitutions and the same phrase is ascribed to Stephen of Muret; but, if the witnesses in the Bologna Canonisation Process are to be trusted, Dominic himself preferred 'To speak about God or with God'. Cf. *AFP* 66 (1996), pp. 71–72.

2 What is said above about the composition and manuscripts of the *Nine Ways* has been supplied by me; in what follows I have adapted and added to Fr Koudelka's comments, which were themselves to some extent inspired by an earlier writing of my own.

3 It is not clear from the Latin whether 'Alatrinus' should be taken as a personal name or as the designation of the bishop's see; in any case, Constantine's story is garbled and he has probably confused the little-known Rinaldo Monaldi (not actually a Cistercian prior), whom Honorius did send to the German king's chancellor, Conrad of Metz, in August 1220, with the better-known legate, Alatrinus. Cf. *AFP* 66 (1996), pp. 51–53.

7 SPEAKING OF GOD

1 This is a possible, if perverse, translation of *Filius hominis qui est in caelo*.

2 This paragraph has been added by me.

3 This account of the founding of Limoges is rather inaccurate, and it was in 1218, not 1217, that Dominic first spoke to Peter about it. Nevertheless the essence of Salanhac's report is entirely credible and can be reconciled with other evidence. Cf. *AFP* 65 (1995), pp. 95–99.

4 Fr Koudelka, in line with the current interpretation, takes this to mean the general chapter; but this is not specified in the text and it seems

intrinsically unlikely that all potential preachers, from anywhere in the order, were expected to be presented to the general chapter. It is far more probable that they would normally be brought before the provincial chapter.

5 As I have argued in *AFP* 66 (1996), pp. 33–46, this interpretation of the bull is most improbable, however traditional it was when Fr Koudelka was writing. It is more likely that the initiative had come from the papal curia, possibly from Cardinal Ugolino, not from Dominic.

6 This text was added to the constitutions some years after Dominic's death, but Dominic had let it be known that he wanted his brethren to have modest buildings.

7 The original Bull, which still exists, clearly has *frumenta doctrine*, which I have translated. Fr Koudelka suggested that *frumenta* was a mistake for *fluenta*, and accordingly translated it 'streams of doctrine'; but it is unlikely that a papal scribe wrote *frumenta* instead of *fluenta*, and *flumenta* (which also means 'streams') is scarcely attested as a Latin word. It seems best to retain the manuscript reading and to accept that the pope's metaphors have become rather confused.

8 This appears to be the correct form of his name, though he is often known as Mannes.

8 DOMINIC AND WOMEN

1 From other evidence it is clear that it was in the course of his general confession, not an exhortation to the brethren, that Dominic admitted his liking for conversation with young women.

2 This must actually mean that she stayed there from All Saints 1221 until the octave of the Ascension 1223. Cf. *AFP* 66 (1996), pp. 144–149.

INDEX AND BIBLIOGRAPHY
OF SOURCES

ABBREVIATIONS

AFP   *Archivum Fratrum Praedicatorum*
ASOP   *Analecta Sacri Ordinis Praedicatorum*
MOPH   *Monumenta Ordinis Praedicatorum Historica*

In what follows, references are given according to paragraph or page numbers in the first published edition to be cited. Numbers in parentheses refer to the numbering of the sources in this edition.

ANONYMOUS CHRONICLE OF THE ORDER

Compiled circa 1254. Edited by B. M. Reichert OP, *MOPH* I, Louvain 1896, pp. 321–338.

  Ed. cit. p. 334　　　　　　　　(67)

BARTHOLOMEW OF TRENT

Liber epilogorum in gesta sanctorum. Written circa 1245. Edited by B. Altaner, *Der hl. Dominikus*, Breslau 1922, pp. 229–239.

17　　　　　　　　　　　　(68)

BERENGARIAN MIRACLES

Compiled on the basis of material collected in response to the general chapter's appeal in 1314. The text is taken from the edition prepared by S. Tugwell OP, shortly to be published in *MOPH*. There is an edition by H. C. Scheeben in *ASOP* 17 (1926), pp. 696–708.

4　　　　　　　　　　　　(95)

BOLOGNA CANONISATION PROCESS

Conducted between 6–18 August 1233. The text is taken from the edition being prepared by S. Tugwell OP. There is an edition by A. Walz OP in *MOPH* XVI, Rome 1935, pp. 118–167. There is an English translation in Lehner, *Saint Dominic*, pp. 99–135; another version is translated in Tugwell, *Early Dominicans*, pp. 66–85.

3　　　　　　　　　(42), (69), (132)
4　　　　　　　　　(43), (133)

5	(15), (59)
6	(21), (134)
7	(30)
8	(60), (65)
11	(104)
12	(44), (66), (105)
13	(70)
17	(151)
20	(48), (71)
21	(28)
22	(27)
24	(139)
25	(33), (72)
26	(87), (140), (152)
27	(16), (143), (153)
28	(49)
29	(22), (168)
31	(37), (73)
32	(32), (74), (106), (154)
33	(23), (61), (135)
35	(155)
36	(94)
37	(31), (75), (136)
38	(47), (156)
41	(29), (76)
42	(50), (77), (157)
43	(34), (107)
46	(24), (78)
47	(108), (137), (158)
48	(19)

CECILIA

Miracula. Dictated probably some time in the early 1280s. The text is taken from the edition being prepared by S. Tugwell OP. There is an edition by A. Walz OP in *AFP* 37 (1967), pp. 5–45. An English translation is included in later editions of Placid Conway's translation of the *Lives of the Brethren*.

1	(181)
2	(182)
11	(35)
13	(180)
14	(183)
15	(1)

CHRONICLE OF ST AGNES, BOLOGNA

Compiled circa 1254. The text is taken from the edition being prepared by S. Tugwell OP. There is an edition by M. G. Cambria OP, *II Monastero Domenicano di S. Agnese in Bologna*, Bologna 1973, pp. 226–231. There is also an edition in *ASOP* 1 (1893–1894), pp. 181–184. A longer extract is translated in Tugwell, *Early Dominicans*, pp. 395–400.

    Ed. cit., pp. 226–228   (184)

CONRAD OF METZ

Letter of 22 April 1221. Edited by V. J. Koudelka in *MOPH* XXV, Rome 1966.

    Ed. cit., pp. 157–158   (150)

CONSTANTINE OF ORVIETO

Legenda S. Dominici. Composed 1244–1246. Edited by H. C. Scheeben in *MOPH* XVI, pp. 261–352.

25	(91)
36	(103)
42	(58)
43	(99)
48	(176)
49	(177)
52	(93)
55	(90)
56	(53)
57	(89)
58	(85)
59	(86)
62	(57)

DOMINIC, ST

Letter to the nuns of Madrid, written in 1220. Edited by S. Tugwell OP in *AFP* 56 (1986), pp. 5–13.

          (178)

FULK, BISHOP OF TOULOUSE

Charter given to St Dominic and his preachers (1215). Edited by V. J. Koudelka OP in *MOPH* XXV, pp. 56–58.

          (131)

HONORIUS III

Letters issued to or for St Dominic and his preachers. Edited by V. J. Koudelka OP in *MOPH* XXV.

19 January 1217 (pp. 76–78)	(166)
21 January 1217 (pp. 78–79)	(147)
11 March 1221 (p. 150)	(149)

Letter of 12 May 1220. Edited by S. Tugwell OP in *AFP* 66 (1996), pp. 169–173.   (148)

HUMBERT OF ROMANS

Legenda S. Dominici. Composed circa 1256. The text is taken from the edition being prepared by S. Tugwell OP. There is an edition by A. Walz OP in *MOPH* XVI, pp. 353–433.

40	(165)

INNOCENT III

Letter of 17 November 1206. Edited by V. J. Koudelka OP in *MOPH* XXV, pp. 11–13.   (127)

JORDAN OF SAXONY

Libellus de Initiis Ordinis Praedicatorum. Written essentially 1219–1221; superficially edited and published early in 1233. The text is taken from the edition being prepared by S. Tugwell OP. There is an edition by H. C. Scheeben in *MOPH* XVI, pp. 1–82. There is an English translation in Lehner, *Saint Dominic*, pp. 5–82; also by Simon Tugwell OP, *Libellus on the Beginnings of the Order of Preachers* (Dominican Sources 1), Dublin and Chicago 1982.

6	(164)
7	(2)
8	(3)
10	(13)
12	(4)
13	(5)
15	(109)
17	(110)
21	(114)
22	(113)
27	(175)
28	(122)
29	(123)
30	(124)

31	(125)
34	(54), (128)
35	(17)
36	(62)
37	(63), (129)
38	(130)
39	(64)
47	(88)
51	(167)
62	(92)
86–87	(161)
92	(174)
103–104	(6)
104	(7)
104–105	(8)
106	(9)
107	(10)
108	(11)

Encyclical of 1233. Edited by Elio Montanari, *B. Iordanis de Saxonia Litterae Encyclicae annis 1233 et 1234 datae*, Florence 1993, pp. 53–73, but the text has been emended by reference to evidence not used by Professor Montanari. There is an English translation in Tugwell, *Early Dominicans*, pp. 122–125, but the Latin text used there was unsatisfactory.

2–3	(12)

LANGUEDOC CANONISATION PROCESS

Conducted in the latter part of August 1233. The text is taken from the edition being prepared by S. Tugwell OP. There is an edition by A. Walz OP in *MOPH* XVI, pp. 173–187, which needs to be supplemented by V. J. Koudelka OP, *AFP* 42 (1972), pp. 61–67. There is an English translation in Lehner, *Saint Dominic*, pp. 137–146.

14	(159)
15	(38), (45)
16	(39)
17	(40)
18	(20), (46), (79), (138)

LIVES OF THE BRETHREN

Gerald de Frachet, *Vitae Fratrum*. Compiled in the late 1250s. Edited by B. M. Reichert in *MOPH* I. There is an English translation by Placid Conway OP, of which the most recent edition was published in London in 1955.

NINE WAYS OF PRAYER OF ST DOMINIC

Compiled in its present form between 1297 and 1308, probably on the basis of older material. The text is taken from a new edition being prepared by S. Tugwell OP. Edited by S. Tugwell OP, *Mediaeval Studies* 47 (1985), pp. 1–124.

PETRUS FERRANDI

Legenda S. Dominici. Composed circa 1235. The text is taken from the edition prepared by S. Tugwell OP. There is an edition by M. H. Laurent OP in *MOPH XVI*, pp. 195–260.

PIERRE DES VAUX-DE-CERNAI

Historia Albigensis (circa 1218). Edited by P. Guébin and E. Lyon, vol. I, Paris 1926.

PRIMITIVE CONSTITUTIONS OF THE ORDER OF PREACHERS

The earliest original legislation was written in 1220, but the oldest surviving text includes alterations and additions made well into the 1230s. The text is based on a study of the manuscripts by S. Tugwell OP. There is an edition by A. H. Thomas OP, *De oudste Constituties van de Dominicanen*, Louvain 1965, pp. 309–369. There is an English translation in Lehner, *Saint Dominic*, pp. 211–251.

Prologue	(169)
I 13	(170)
II 20	(145)
II 23	(171)
II 26	(162)
II 28	(172)
II 29	(173)
II 31	(144)
II 33	(146)
II 35	(163)

PUYLAURENS, GUILLAUME DE

Chronica (circa 1275). Edited by J. Duvernoy, Paris 1976.

8	(119)

RODRIGO DE CERRATO

Vatae sanctorum (third recension). Compiled in the early 1270s. The text is taken from an edition of the *Vita S. Dominici* being prepared by S. Tugwell OP. There is an edition of the life of St Dominic by T. M. Mamachi OP, *Annalium Ordinis Praedicatorum volumen primum*, Rome 1756, Appendix cols. 312–334. There is also an edition (without paragraph numbers) by V. D. Carro OP, *Domingo de Guzmán*, Madrid 1973, pp. 775–801.

4	(14)

STEPHEN OF BOURBON

Tractatus de diversis materiis praedicabilibus. Compiled probably circa 1250–1260. A selection was edited by A. Lecoy de la Marche, *Anecdotes historiques, légendes et apologues tirés du receuil inédit d'Étienne de Bourbon*, Paris 1877. The paragraph numbers are taken from this edition. A complete edition by Jacques Berlioz is due to be published in the series *Corpus Christianorum*.

83	(115)
158	(179)

STEPHEN OF SALANHAC

De quatuor in quibus Deus praedicatorum ordinem insignivit. Salanhac abandoned his compilation unfinished in 1278; it was edited and amplified by Bernard Gui in the early fourteenth century. Ed. Thomas Kaeppeli OP, *MOPH* XXII, Rome 1949.

I 7	(141)
I 8	(142)
I 9	(81)
III 7:8	(160)

GENERAL BIBLIOGRAPHY

Bedouelle, Guy, OP: *Saint Dominic: The Grace of the Word*, San Francisco 1987.

Cahill, Barbara, OP: *Dominic the Preacher*, London 1988.

Gallén, Jarl: 'Les voyages de saint Dominique au Danemark. Essai de datation' in Raymund Creytens and Pius Künzle OP eds, *Xenia Medii Aevi Historiam Illustrantia oblata Thomae Kaeppeli OP*, Rome 1978, pp. 73–84.

Koudelka, Vladimir J., OP: 'Les dépositions des témoins au procès de canonisation de saint Dominique', *AFP* 42 (1972), pp. 47–67.

Koudelka, Vladimir J., OP: 'Le "Monasterium Tempuli" et la fondation dominicaine de San Sisto', *AFP* 31 (1961), pp. 5–81.

Koudelka, Vladimir J., OP: 'Notes sur le cartulaire de S. Dominique', *AFP* 28 (1958), pp. 92–114, 33 (1963), pp. 89–120, 34 (1964), pp. 5–44.

Koudelka, Vladimir J., OP: 'Notes pour servir à l'histoire de saint Dominique', *AFP* 35 (1965), pp. 5–20, 43 (1973), pp. 5–27.

Lehner, Francis C., OP: *Saint Dominic, Biographical Documents*, Washington DC 1964.

Tugwell, Simon, OP: 'Dominic the Founder', *Dominican Ashram* 4 (1985), pp. 80–96, 122–145.

Tugwell, Simon, OP: *Early Dominicans*, Classics of Western Spirituality, New York 1982.

Tugwell, Simon, OP: 'Friars and Canons: the earliest Dominicans' in Judith Loades, ed., *Monastic Studies II*, Headstart History, Bangor 1991, pp. 193–207.

Tugwell, Simon, OP: *Saint Dominic*, Strasbourg 1995.

Tugwell, Simon, OP: 'Notes on the life of St Dominic', *AFP* 65 (1995), pp. 5–169; 66 (1996), pp. 5–200.

Vicaire, M.-H., OP: *The Genius of St Dominic*, Nagpur 1990.

Vicaire, M.-H., OP: *Histoire de Saint Dominique* (revised edition), Paris 1982. There is an English translation of the first edition of this work, *Saint Dominic and his Times*, London 1964.